Acclaim for Eric Alterman's

It Ain't No Sin to Be Glad You're Alive
The Promise of Bruce Springsteen

"No mere book can take the place of a ticket to Bruce's recent sold-out tour, but *It Ain't No Sin to Be Glad You're Alive* might be the next best thing. . . . For someone who would like to know what it is about New Jersey's favorite son that fascinates and inspires such fervent devotion, *It Ain't No Sin* is as eloquent and sweet a testament as you're likely to find."

—*Maxim*

"What a nice surprise to be treated to a uniquely absorbing book on Springsteen. . . . Eric Alterman's *It Ain't No Sin to Be Glad You're Alive* succeeds where no other Springsteen bio has by capturing the singer's appeal without merely stringing together old anecdotes. . . . Alterman dutifully takes readers back to Springsteen's New Jersey childhood and depicts the singer's strained relationship with his dad without resorting to 'Behind the Music'–style sensationalism. He then follows young Bruce through his early career battles and ultimate triumph in the music industry, setting the scene for the breakthrough album 'Born to Run' and its mixed blessing in the songwriter's life. . . . Alterman later captures the complexities of the 'Born in the U.S.A.' era with unmatched insight. Not only does the author appraise the work and its commercial concessions fairly, he skillfully connects the album with its unique political and social settings, arguing effectively on behalf of Springsteen's integrity without sounding like a blind fan. . . . Alterman is fair and eloquent in his appraisal of Springsteen's discography. . . . Most important, Alterman shows noble restraint in his discussion of Springsteen's private life. While he certainly doesn't shy away from the artist's troubled childhood or failed first marriage, the author treats the fragile subject matter properly and avoids painting the singer's down moments with a melodramatic brush. Ultimately, he portrays Springsteen as a real person." —*Billboard*

"Clever . . . persuasive . . . intelligent."
—John D. Thomas, *New York Times Book Review*

"A well-researched, passionate, musicologically informed and politically astute appreciation of the great rock 'n' roll artist." —E. L. Doctorow

"Alterman deploys biographical detail sparingly but well, always to the purpose: elucidating his subject's extraordinary body of work, which comprises not only hundreds of songs but also thousands of strenuous, exhilarating live performances. . . . This concise, passionate appreciation of the dominant rock musician of his generation . . . makes a case for Springsteen's importance as a chronicler of social pain and, through his music, a creator of community: in this persuasive portrait, Springsteen is a mature artist quite consciously guided by a sense of responsibility to his audience, his country, and his own talent."   —*The New Yorker*

"A seasoned political journalist and a fervent Bruce Springsteen fan, Alterman crafts a balanced yet passionate bio that plumbs the Boss's artistic origins and achievements."   —*People*

"Springsteen is one of the few artists of the last half century who can be called truly original. He looms so large on the landscape of popular music that I am surprised that this book wasn't written before now. *It Ain't No Sin to Be Glad You're Alive* is fascinating, well researched and serious: three qualities not often found together in biographies of musicians. It ranks with Peter Guralnick's work and is an essential document in evaluating Springsteen's legacy."   —Rosanne Cash

It Ain't No Sin to Be Glad You're Alive

It Ain't No Sin to Be Glad You're Alive

The Promise of Bruce Springsteen

Eric Alterman

 Little, Brown and Company

BOSTON | NEW YORK | LONDON

ALSO BY ERIC ALTERMAN

Who Speaks for America? Why Democracy Matters in Foreign Policy (1998)

Sound and Fury: The Making of the Punditocracy (1992 and 1999)

Originally published in hardcover
by Little, Brown and Company, October 1999

First Back Bay paperback edition, August 2001

Library of Congress Cataloging-in-Publication Data
Alterman, Eric.
    It ain't no sin to be glad you're alive : the promise of Bruce
Springsteen / Eric Alterman. — 1st. ed.
        p.   cm.
    Includes bibliographical references.
    ISBN 0-316-03885-7 (hc) / 0-316-03917-9 (pb)
    1. Springsteen, Bruce.   2. Rock musicians — United States
Biography.   I. Title.
ML420.S77A65   1999
782.42166'092 — dc21
[B]   99-38539

10   9   8   7   6   5   4   3   2   1

Q-FF

Printed in the United States of America

Contents

TO EVE ROSE ALTERMAN

Born to run on April 6, 1998

*"In a world so hard and dirty, so fouled and confused
Searching for a little bit of God's mercy, I found living proof."*

It Ain't No Sin to Be Glad You're Alive

Introduction

On a rainy late-November afternoon in 1998, I shook hands with Bruce Springsteen. We were introduced by his manager and coproducer, Jon Landau, in the Green Room of *The Charlie Rose Show*. I was there because I had called Charlie earlier in the day and asked if I could show up for Bruce's interview. I had been a guest on his show a few times, and we were friendly in a dinner/cocktail party kind of way, and as Charlie is a nice guy, he said sure. And so that afternoon I was ushered into a little room where Bruce was sitting alone with his acoustic guitar.

Landau, who arrived at the same time, came in with me, and said something complimentary about my political writing to Bruce. Looking tan and rested, Bruce stood up from the table to shake my hand and told me he was "real glad" to meet me. I had been imagining this moment for nearly a quarter century but I still hadn't figured out what to say. During the past twenty-five years, I had driven hundreds of miles, flown across oceans, waited on overnight ticket lines, lied to my parents and professors, bribed bouncers, flattered girls I wasn't so crazy about, and worse, to see this man perform. But I was a grown-up now. I didn't want to gush; I didn't want to sound like every other smitten fan in the world whose life Bruce had changed. I believed in the art, I reminded myself, not the artist. Still, I wanted to be honest. There were any number of times since I had turned fifteen when I had felt as if Bruce were somehow saving my life. He had proved the one constant between my adolescence and my adulthood, between my being the son of my father and the father of my daughter. He had been a source of hope and inspiration, of friendship and fortitude, of therapy and solidarity, of consolation and exhilaration. He still was.

So what did I say? Not much, it turned out. I figured he'd heard it all before, and what good would it do, when, really, all he wanted to do was prepare for his interview. I didn't ask for his autograph or try to prolong the conversation artificially. I decided instead to maintain my dignity and simply thank him for "everything" without going into too much detail about just how much I wanted that word to contain. We shook hands again and I left. An hour later, when the interview was over and Bruce came back into the Green Room, I handed him his guitar, and he went out before the cameras to play a blistering acoustic version of "Born in the U.S.A." When the song ended, he said good-bye, we shook hands one more time, and Bruce quickly headed down a secret elevator to a waiting Town Car.

Here's what I wanted to say . . .

Now every man has the right to live

The right to a chance to give what he has to give

The right to fight for the things that he believes

For the things that come to him in dreams.

— Bruce Springsteen, in a verse he added to Elvis Presley's "Follow
   That Dream"*

* The song was actually composed by Ben Weisman and Fred Wise for the
1961 movie of the same name.

Follow That Dream

Lenny Kaye, the rock archivist and guitarist with the Patti Smith Group, has boiled down the essential myth of rock 'n' roll as follows: "In the either/or mythos of teenagery, you either hang with the quasi-thugs or the bespectacled intellectuals, the jocks or the jokesters. But what if your developing personality doesn't fit with such preconceived notions — or even odder than odd, you move between both polarities, a mutation on par with the paired opposites? . . . Why then, you form a band. Find a bunch of other misfits and start playing the music that still other misfits pass along."

Bruce Springsteen is the mythos of rock 'n' roll sprung to life. During his quarter-century career as a recording artist, any number of commentators, beginning with one for the *New York Times* in 1975, have voiced the complaint that "if there hadn't been a Bruce Springsteen,

then critics would have made him up."* The argument
is exactly backwards: the problem with Bruce Springsteen was not that he was a critic's invention; rather, it
was that he was too good to be true. No responsible
writer would dare invent him.

Beginning in 1963, when fourteen-year-old Bruce
Springsteen walked into Freehold's Western Auto Store
and handed over the eighteen dollars he had saved
housepainting, roof tarring, and gardening for his first
real guitar, the boy had pursued his dream with a degree
of relentlessness that makes Captain Ahab seem a Gen X
slacker by comparison. He was a loner and something
of a social leper. His face was scarred with acne, and
his personality crippled by shyness. He was teased
and abused at school, first by nuns and later by his
classmates. He was on the receiving end of little but
barely muted rage from his father. He grew up in a house
with no books, where "art," he later said, was "twenty
minutes in school every day that you hate." But the
house did have a radio atop the kitchen refrigerator,
and through the magic of the music inside that radio,
Bruce Springsteen found what for him was the key to
the universe: he was going to make the kind of music
that liberated his young soul from the prison of a mis-
fit Jersey adolescence, or he was going to die trying.
And, wonder of wonders, he did it and somehow man-

---

* Henry Edwards, *New York Times* Arts and Leisure section, October 5,
1975, p. 1. The British critic Simon Frith repeated the formula almost word
for word in 1987, adding only the modifier *American* to the word *critics*.

aged to bring a few million of the rest of us along for the ride.

The story of Bruce Springsteen's childhood recalls a bad Dickens novel written with the Who's *Quadrophenia* playing in the background. Though the surname is Dutch, Bruce Springsteen was born in Freehold, New Jersey, on September 23, 1949, the firstborn child of Irish and Italian parents. His father, Douglas, was an embittered man who struggled to find a place for himself in the local economy. He worked, for brief periods, in the local rug mill, as a jail guard, and as a cab and bus driver. He had no friends; not one person, claimed Bruce, came to visit his father in twenty years.

Bruce's home life was dark and oppressive, filled with menacing authority. His relationship with his father involved little but discipline and rebellion. As Bruce ruefully recalled in concert, "When I was growing up, there were two things that were unpopular in my house: one was me, the other was my guitar." He has joked about his father's apparent belief that his guitar was manufactured by a company called Goddamn, as in "turn down that Goddamn guitar." When Bruce would practice alone in his room, his father would turn on the gas jets on the stove and direct them into the heating ducts that led to the boy's bedroom in an attempt to drive his son out.

According to Bruce, his father especially used to enjoy needling him when young men were being killed in Vietnam at a prodigious rate: "I can't wait until the army gets you. When the army gets you, they gonna make a man of you. They gonna cut off all that hair, and they'll make a man of you." (Though he did express relief when his son succeeded in failing his draft-board physical.) Once, according to a typical early father-son concert monologue, Bruce suffered a motorcycle accident and was briefly laid up in bed. Douglas Springsteen took the opportunity to call in a barber to cut off Bruce's hair. "I can remember telling my dad that I hated him and I would never ever forget it," Springsteen would tell the crowd.

Springsteen has said he "did a lot of running away and a lot of being brought back. It was always . . . very terrible." Often he would take the bus to Manhattan and try to spend the night at the Port Authority bus station. When the police would call his parents, it was always his mother who showed up to pick him up. At home, his father would sit alone in the kitchen drinking beer and smoking cigarettes, waiting for his son to come home with all the lights in the house turned off. The only visible light would be the smoldering ember from his father's cigarette, which Bruce could see through the screen door. Sometimes Bruce would try to wait him out in the driveway, next door to Ducky Slattery's Sinclair station, slicking his hair back in a futile attempt to conceal its length. Sometimes he would go in, and the two would argue about Bruce's hair, his attitude, his future. "Pretty soon," as Bruce told it, "we'd end up screaming at each other, and my mother would come running up from the front room, trying to pull him off me, trying to keep us from fighting with each other. And I'd always end up running out the back door screaming, telling him . . . that it was my life and I could do what I wanted to do." (Springsteen used to tell this story before launching into his version of the Animals' "It's My Life.")

Adele Springsteen worked as a legal secretary. She took pride in her professional identity and remained in the same job for Bruce's entire childhood. To Bruce, she "was just like Superwoman. She did everything, everywhere, all the time." At night his mother would "set her hair and she would come downstairs and just turn on the TV till she fell asleep. And then she'd get up the next morning and do it again."

Springsteen's deep affection for his mother is immortalized in his song "The Wish," which may be the only great mother-love song written outside the realm of country-and-western music. When Bruce was sixteen, Adele, who worked for minimum wage, took out a sixty-dollar loan to buy her son "a brand-new Japanese [electric] guitar." He found it, a "barely tunable" Kent guitar with a small amplifier, "lying underneath . . . a Christmas tree [that] shines one beautiful star," and the moment remains one of the only happy childhood memories that have found their way into Springsteen's writing. Sixty dollars, Bruce remembered, "was more money than I [had] ever seen in one place in my life." Because the finance company was located just around the corner from the family's home, Bruce had to watch his mother go in and make those payments on the loan every single week. "It was a very defining moment, standing in front of the music store with someone who's going to do everything she can to give you what you needed that day, and having the faith that you were going to make sense of it," he later explained. Douglas and Adele Springsteen also had two daughters, Virginia, born in 1950, and Pamela, born in 1962. While they did not figure heavily in Springsteen's earlier work, he speaks today with considerable love and affection whenever either one's name comes up.

The Springsteens lived in a lower-middle-class section of Freehold called Texas, where a group of Appalachian refugees had come together with a smattering of white ethnics in one of America's less publicized migrations. The 1939 *WPA Guide to New Jersey* observes of the town that "in an unobtrusive way it seems to embody America's growth from farm to factory." Yet Freehold was largely bypassed by the prosperity enjoyed by much of white America in the 1950s and 1960s. Most of the available work came from the local 3M factory, a rug mill, a Nescafé factory, and a number of much smaller manufacturers. Deeply segregated, Freehold's whites and blacks lived, respectively, on the "right" and "wrong" side of an actual railroad track. To Bruce, his hometown was "a small, narrow-minded town . . . very conservative . . . stagnating. . . . There really wasn't much." With the distance of more than a generation, he later sang

Follow That Dream

I got outta here, yeah, hard and fast in Freehold
Back then everybody wanted to kick my ass in
  Freehold
Well, if you were different, black or brown,
It could be a pretty redneck town
Yeah, Freehold.

The distancing irony Springsteen usually employs to talk about his childhood can turn to bitter anger on the topic of the nuns who were his teachers. "I hated school. I had the big hate," he said in 1978. In the third grade a nun stuffed Bruce into a garbage can she kept under her desk, because, he said, "she told me that's where I belonged." He also had the distinction of being the only altar boy knocked down by a priest on the steps of the altar during Mass. In eighth grade, after "wising off," Bruce was sent down to the first-grade class, where he was forced to sit at a desk made for a child a fraction of his size. When he accidentally smiled at the nun who forced him into the tiny seat, she turned to one of the students and commanded, "Show this young man what we do to people who smile in this classroom." To young Bruce's horror and amazement, "This kid, this six-year-old who has no doubt been taught to do this, he comes over to me — him standing up and me sitting in this little desk — and he slams me in the face. I can still feel the sting."

The following year Bruce demanded to go to public high school, which, because it had been integrated, was shunned by virtually all students whose parents could afford an alternative. The reaction, he explained, was rather dramatic. "Freehold Regional . . . it was like 'Are you insane? You are dirt! You are the worst! You are a barbarian!'" At high school Bruce participated in no activities, sports, or even much in the way of academics. One of his teachers even suggested to his classmates that, for the sake of their own "self-respect," Bruce not be allowed to graduate, given the indecency of his long hair. "I didn't even make it to class clown. I had nowhere near that amount of notoriety," he later recalled. "I didn't have, like, the flair to be the complete jerk. It was like I didn't exist. It was the wall, then me." One high school classmate concurred: "If he hadn't turned out to be Bruce Springsteen, would I remember him? I can't think of why I would. You have to remember, without a guitar in his hands, he had absolutely nothing to say."

Springsteen's formal education finally ended after a short period at Ocean County Community College. He arrived there in his standard uniform — a Fruit of the Loom undershirt, tight jeans, sneakers, and leather jacket — and was rapidly invited into a counselor's office for a friendly tête-à-tête. As Springsteen told the story to a reporter, the meeting went as follows:

"You've got trouble at home, right?"

"Look, things are great. I feel fine," Springsteen replied warily.

"Then why do you look like that?"

"What are you talking about?"

"There are some students who have . . . complained about you."

"Well, that's their problem, you know?" said Springsteen, ending both the conversation and his personal commitment to higher education.

Like the character Jenny in the Velvet Underground's anthem, young Bruce Springsteen's "life was saved by rock 'n' roll." Describing himself alternately as "nowhere," "on the outs," "weird," a "loser," "living in a trance," and "dead," Bruce rescued himself by buying a guitar and teaching himself how to play. "My first guitar was one of the most beautiful sights I'd ever seen in my life," he remembered. "It was a magic scene. . . . It was real and it stood for something. 'Now you're real.'" In a 1974 interview Bruce explained that he had "tried to play football and baseball and all those things. I checked out all the alleys and just didn't fit. Music gave me something. I was running through a maze. It was never just a hobby. It was a reason to live." Tellingly, Springsteen observed, "The first day I can remember looking in a mirror and being able to stand what I was seeing was the day I had a guitar in my hand."

Inspired initially by seeing Elvis, and later the Beatles, on *The Ed Sullivan Show*, Bruce remembered experiencing some "shock" of recognition even at that young age. "I was nine years old when I saw Elvis on *Ed Sullivan*, and I had to get a guitar the next day. I stood in front of my mirror with that guitar on . . . and I knew that that's what I had been missing." But at nine Bruce was too young to learn to play. Later, after hearing Elvis, the Beatles, the Stones, Roy Orbison, and the old-time soul and R&B singers who predated them, Bruce felt "a sense of wonderment" that furnished "both the dream and the direct channel through which I could fulfill that dream." Rock, he would note later in interviews, "provided me with a community, filled with people, and brothers and sisters who I didn't know, but who I knew were out there. We had this enormous thing in common, this 'thing' that initially felt like a secret . . . a home where my spirit could wander. . . . It was the liberating thing, the out . . . my connection to the rest of the human race." No less important for Bruce, who was constantly losing battles to the arbitrary authority of his father and nasty nuns, was the promise of a land where a young man could stand his ground. "Rock 'n' roll was never, never about surrender."

The music likewise "reached down into all those homes where there was no music or books or any kind of creative sense, and it infiltrated the whole thing. It was like the voice of America, the real America coming into your home." To say rock 'n' roll was the "only culture" Bruce knew is no overstatement. Springsteen was hardly exaggerating when later he sang that he learned "more from a three-minute record than he ever learned in school." As a teenager, Bruce managed to hear what he understood to be "tremendous depth and sadness in the voice of the singer singing 'Saturday Night at the Movies'" — an otherwise forgettable song about, what else, going to the movies. His cultural and emotional deprivation made Bruce hungrier when it came to ingesting the coded messages of rebellion, passion, power, and sex that rock had to offer. When it came his turn onstage, he wanted to capture all of it at once. Bruce Springsteen did not particularly care for rock stardom. He wanted to make music that would save lives.

While he accepted the frivolousness of most of rock's subject matter, he was, when it came to rock 'n' roll, decidedly a serious young man. Bruce understood that rock should be "fun — dancing, screwing, having a good time, but . . . I also believed it was capable of conveying serious ideas and that the people who listened to it, whatever you want to call them, were looking for something."

When one considers the emotional pain with which Bruce associated both home and school, coupled with his minimal social life, one begins to understand the degree of obsession with which he approached music. "A lot of rock 'n' roll people," he has noted, "that's where they came from, just this solitary existence. If you're gonna be good at something, you gotta be alone a lot to practice, there has to be a certain involuntariness to it." As a teenage musician, Springsteen showed the kind of self-possession and sense of purpose that are usually associated with high school valedictorians and National Merit Scholars. He never smoked a joint and rarely took a drink. Bruce estimated that as a kid, from the time he first figured out Keith Richards's lead on "It's All Over

Now" (his first song), he practiced six to eight hours at a time, every night. At the school dances, he "was the guy standing with his arms folded in front of the guitar player, all night long." He recognized that music was "something that I was going to have to work at very hard to do well."

Bruce joined his first band about six months after buying the guitar. According to Tex Vinyard, a colorful Freehold resident who mentored young musicians, a pimply teenager showed up on his doorstep "one night [when] it was raining like cows pissin' on a flat rock." Bruce's career began when he asked to be the guitarist in the one-amplifier teenage band that Tex and his wife, Marion, were then sponsoring. When Tex asked him what songs he could play, Bruce said he didn't know any, so Tex told him to come back when he had learned five. The next night, while the band was practicing at the Vinyard home, Tex recalled, "there's a knock on the door. 'Hi. I'm Bruce Springsteen, remember me?'" The boy had mastered the lead guitar line on five songs by copying what he had heard on the radio during the past twenty-four hours. "Does this make us friends?" asked young Bruce. It certainly did — at least according to Tex's version, which Bruce has said "is better than reality," though "almost exactly the way it happened."

The Vinyards got rid of most of the furniture in their living room to give the boys a place to practice. But when the band's first gig approached, they still had no professional equipment. All its members came from homes with no money, and Tex himself was already try-ing to make it on twenty-one-dollars-a-week strike pay, having borrowed, he said, $1,200 on a car. Following weeks of consistent badgering by the boys, Tex finally walked over to the music store and came home with a three-hundred-dollar amplifier with four inputs, for which he put five dollars down. Bruce Springsteen's first gig ever — in 1965, at the Woodhaven Swim Club — ended with a Bruce-arranged version of Glenn Miller's "In the Mood." His band, the Castiles, dressed in faux Beatle outfits and received thirty-five-dollars; the boys insisted that Tex accept his $3.50 management fee. The group recorded a demo in the shopping center of the Bricktown Mall in May of 1966, and enjoyed the thrill of playing Cafe Wha? in Greenwich Village, where, accord-ing to Tex, they were witnessed by members of the Ras-cals and the Lovin' Spoonful. Thirty years later, at the 1999 Rock and Roll Hall of Fame induction ceremony, Springsteen would thank Tex, who was deceased, and Marion, who was present, for "open[ing] up their home to a bunch of rock 'n' roll misfits and let[ting] us make a lot of noise and practice all night long."

Even as a teenager, Bruce was not one to compromise what he believed to be the integrity of his music. Spring-steen refused to play Top 40 material with his earliest bands — the kind of music the other kids wanted to dance to — in favor of his own originals and obscure soul and R&B songs that he felt were worthy. Moreover, his sound fit into neither the surf music in fashion on the shore nor the retro-rock favored among bikers and greasers in the tough-guy bars. Bruce's earliest bands played at the Elks Club, the Roller-drome, Sing Sing, and the local insane asylum, which the boys found more disconcerting than the prison. "We were always terrified at the asylum," Bruce explained. "One time this guy in a suit got up and introduced us for twenty minutes, sayin' we were greater than the Beatles. Then the doctors came up and took him away."

Following their own American Dream, the Springsteens gave up on New Jersey when Bruce was just eighteen and moved to California in the hopes of a better life. Bruce stayed behind in his parents' house but left within a month of their departure and spent the next five years crashing wherever he could. Amazingly, given one of his most obsessive themes, Bruce had not yet learned to drive. Meanwhile, his living arrangements alternated between rooms above an out-of-business beauty parlor (where he wrote much of *Greetings from Asbury Park*) and the shared digs in a surfboard factory inside an industrial park, owned by Carl "Tinker" West, who eventually replaced Tex Vinyard as the young man's mentor. Bruce's drummer, Vini Lopez, slept in one bathroom of Tinker's store, while keyboardist Danny Federici slept in another. "It was tough," Bruce remembered, "because the resin from the surfboards really knocked you out for a while. But it allowed me to spend time working on my music."

With little to tie Bruce to Freehold, his life revolved

around the dilapidated blue-collar resort town of Asbury Park, located sixty miles south of New York City. In its glory days, the ornate palaces near its boardwalk hosted the likes of Sinatra, Billie Holiday, and the Marx Brothers. In later decades, a teenage Bruce Springsteen caught a Doors' performance there, and saw the Who smash their guitars onstage (going up to the stage to search for salvage afterward). While today, with its rotting boardwalk and blighted landscape, Asbury Park may look, as Ron Rosenbaum has observed, "like frozen death," back in the early seventies its demise remained an open question. Although a bitter race riot in 1970 had destroyed the town's potential as a resort, by then it had little to offer tourists: tacky hotels, cheap diners, a quaint Ferris wheel, and a narrow strip of beach eroding beside an equally narrow boardwalk. After the riots, families that could afford it took their vacations elsewhere, and Main Street was all but shuttered and the town's two hundred hotels dwindled down to one. Crime, drugs, and the accoutrements of urban decay eventually replaced the disappearing vacationers.

What did survive was its gritty, urban, and racially mongrelized music scene. In the early seventies, recalls Southside Johnny, "we had twenty or thirty clubs in a twenty-mile radius." Blues, jazz, and R&B cooked themselves into a musical stew that was unique to the area and rather insulated from musical developments in, say, New York or Philadelphia, to say nothing of San Francisco or southern California.

The Upstage Club on Cookman Avenue, located two flights above a Thom McAn shoe store, was the place where all the area's young musicians honed their craft. Through the haze of historical memory, the club has taken on a kind of iconographic status, not unlike Sylvia Beach's Paris bookstore, or Sam Phillips's Sun studio in Memphis. It was at the Upstage where Bruce forged his lifetime friendship with guitarist and musical alter ego, "Miami" Steve Van Zandt, along with the likes of "Southside" Johnny Lyon, E Street Band members "Phantom" Danny Federici and Garry W. Tallent, and E Street alumnus "Mad Dog" Vini Lopez. As Bruce would later write in the liner notes to Southside Johnny's first album: "That club brought out everybody's talents." The kids at the Upstage were "each in their own way a living spirit of what, to me, rock 'n' roll is all about. It was music as survival, and they lived it down in their souls, night after night. The guys were their own heroes and they never forgot." Later in life Springsteen would trace his earliest appreciation of the concept of community — "a community of ideas and values" — to "an extension of that thing you felt in a bar on Saturday night in Asbury Park when it was just a hundred and fifty people in the room."

The raunchy, raucous club, operated by Tom and Margaret Potter, was decorated with psychedelic, Day-Glo nudie posters and was equipped with high-powered amplifiers so that musicians could show up with just a guitar and jam. The Upstage stayed open from eight in the evening until five in the morning (with a one-hour break at midnight to clear out the minors), which meant that musicians could basically live there at night and crash on the beach during the day. The favored musicians were actual "club members," who were allowed in whenever they wished without paying. In return, they were expected to put together a band at a moment's notice and just get on stage and start jamming with whomever was in the room. The club occupied two floors, one for folk/acoustic types and one for rock, jazz, and blues musicians. Bruce played both floors and was, according to a former member, "the main man out front. A lot of things revolved around him." One musician at the time compared the transformation that the shy, inarticulate boy underwent when stepping on stage to that of "the Incredible Hulk. Put him onstage with a guitar, and he lit it up. It was like somebody had plugged him in."

While the Upstage operated on the timeless no hero, no class rules of all bohemia, it was clear to most that one of its denizens was living a larger destiny than the rest. As Garry Tallent later recalled, "If there was any chance of us making a living through music, we figured it would have to happen through Bruce." Another musician remembered the experience of jamming with Springsteen as "like having Einstein coming over and doing your homework for you." It was as a result of his unique status at the club that Springsteen first became saddled with the horribly inappropriate nickname "the Boss." (Springsteen detested the nickname. "I hate bosses. I hate being called the Boss," he has complained).

Springsteen's first band of any repute was called Steel Mill, and included Vini Lopez on drums, Danny Federici on keyboards, and Steve Van Zandt on guitar, all members of the future E Street Band. Bruce described its style as "basically a riff-oriented hard-rock thing" in the mold of Cream or early Led Zeppelin. Surviving tapes document a band of genuine originality but limited musicianship and melodic content. Still, they developed an extremely large following along the Shore, so perhaps they were better than they sound today. After a cross-country road trip in January 1970, the band landed a gig as an opener at the Matrix in San Francisco. A reviewer for the *San Francisco Examiner*, Philip Elwood, was so impressed by a January 13 performance that he ignored the headliners and reviewed Steel Mill instead. He wrote that he had "never been so overwhelmed by totally unknown talent" and called Steel Mill "the first big thing that's happened to Asbury Park since the good ship *Morro Castle* burned to the waterline of that Jersey beach in '34." Although the band unfortunately failed an audition to be the headliner at the famed Family Dog Ballroom, it did cut a demo for the impresario Bill Graham but Tinker refused his $1,000 offer of a contract. Eventually, they ran out of money and patience, and Bruce came home to Asbury Park that winter on the back of a flatbed truck. Steel Mill soon collapsed, and the rest of its members sought gainful employment. Not

Bruce. He would take the bus up to Greenwich Village and play solo gigs for his food money, writing a new song or two on each leg of the journey.

Springsteen's next major musical venture was the legendary Dr. Zoom and the Sonic Boom. More a traveling carnival than a band, the group was a remarkably democratic institution, featuring people who played no instrument but remained in the band as twirlers or Monopoly players. ("Yeah, I'm in Dr. Zoom. I play Monopoly" went the saying.) One of the Boom even repaired an engine on stage, wearing a tuxedo. It was an early form of performance art, and though the band opened for the Allman Brothers once, they could hardly sustain the level of chaos they generated. Among the thirty or so band members were Bruce, Steve Van Zandt, Gary W. Tallent, Danny Federici, and Southside Johnny. Typical pay for a gig was about five dollars per performer. It may have been fun, but it was no living.

Dr. Zoom eventually morphed into the Bruce Springsteen Band, featuring Van Zandt, Federici, Tallent, and David Sancious, a talented jazz musician who would play keyboards for the original, pre–*Born to Run* E Street Band. The ten-member group, including horns and three black female backup singers, was Bruce's first genuine artistic breakthrough, dedicated primarily to performing Springsteen originals, which were growing increasingly sophisticated. The band began to coalesce around an early seventies hard-rock sound, featuring important touches of Brill Building pop and Philadelphia soul, that was both unique and compelling. Its version of Bruce's "You Mean So Much to Me," played at Damrosch Park in New York City in the summer of 1971, and later recorded by Southside Johnny and Ronnie Spector, is a timeless piece of danceable pop craftsmanship. What's more, Bruce's lyrics were developing a touch of both humor and social commentary. At a January 1971 gig at the Scene in Asbury Park, Bruce demonstrated an ability to mock the pretensions of Woodstock Nation bands like the Jefferson Airplane and Country Joe and the Fish with lyrics that advised listeners to "Break out the guns and the ammo," and to "Take LSD and off the pigs." Summer, he sang, was over, and the revolution had arrived, and they were "gonna have ourselves a real good time." Over Bruce's vocals the band members cried, "Whoa, whoa, it's revolution," and, "Hey, hey, it's revolution!"

The first night the band played the Student Prince on Kingsley Avenue in Asbury Park, they were offered all the receipts from the door and ended up splitting fifteen dollars ten ways. But they soon developed a considerable local reputation and a dedicated following, sometimes drawing as many as three thousand people to a single gig. The Bruce Springsteen Band became the house band at the Upstage and played there every Friday, Saturday, and Sunday night to the club's capacity of 180 people, with the line three or four deep at the door. By virtually all contemporary accounts, they were among the greatest anonymous, unrecorded bands in the history of pop music. Robert Santelli, currently education director at the

Rock and Roll Hall of Fame in Cleveland, caught one of the band's final performances there, just before Springsteen went off on his recording career, in early 1972. According to Santelli, "By the time he jumped into his rollicking version of 'Jambalaya,' all of us at the Student Prince were wedged between the stage and the few tables and chairs on the perimeter of the dance floor. With a fury of horns and soul shouts that would have impressed Wilson Pickett or even James Brown, the band climaxed with a twin-guitar solo shoot-out — Springsteen versus Miami Steve — that temporarily transformed the Student Prince into the center of the rock 'n' roll universe, with Springsteen as its ruler."

In the coming years, that universe expanded as its center exploded. Cinderella found her rock 'n' roll shoes.

I had skin like leather and the

    diamond-hard look of a cobra

I was born blue and weathered

    but I burst just like a supernova

I could walk like Brando right into the sun

Then dance just like a Casanova

— "It's Hard to Be a Saint in the City," 1973

A Saint in the City

As most of us are eventually forced to admit, romantic ideals of bohemian poverty tend to die unromantic deaths in the face of hunger pangs. Following a few years of living for the thrill of making great rock 'n' roll, most members of Steel Mill, Dr. Zoom, the Bruce Springsteen Band, and the Upstage Club drifted into day jobs, college, domesticity, and other obligations. As Bruce later put it, "The kicks started to wear off. A lot of the time we didn't make enough to eat. That was why I signed with Mike [Appel]. Anything was better than what was happening at the time."

At that critical moment in Springsteen history, Appel and Bruce looked to be the perfect match. Bruce, at twenty-one, was still so shy offstage that he could barely communicate. Appel, twenty-six, on the other hand, was a fast-talking, big-dreaming schemer, an ex-marine whose singular achievement in pop music till then had been composing a hit single for the Partridge Family. In discovering Bruce — this explosive, unfocused talent, emotionally immature and wholly unconcerned about money — he could hardly believe his good fortune. As Appel later recalled it, the first time he heard Bruce sing "It's Hard to Be a Saint in the City," he insisted that Springsteen run through the song again, just to make sure he wasn't imagining it. *Why me, Lord?* Appel said he asked himself. "I'm a guy with all this candy-assed pop commercial kind of records that I've been involved with all my life, like the Partridge Family. Why would I get a guy like this?" But if Bruce was going to be Elvis, then Mike Appel was more than happy to serve as Colonel Tom Parker.

"Everyone was freshly scrubbed, just like it was supposed to be," Appel remembered. It was early 1972, and once again, the rock 'n' roll fairy tale cast itself at perfect pitch: the man-child with nothing but talent meets the promoter with street smarts and tireless drive but little in the way of real-world experience. Bruce had just returned from a trip to California with Tinker West, where he tried and failed to make a reputation for himself as a solo artist. "There were too many good musicians," he remembered, and he had left his "'bar band king' rep in Jersey." So the hungry young man signs a "rinky-dink" contract (in Appel's words), literally on the hood of a car, which amounts to indentured servitude, entitling the manager to an exorbitant percentage of the artist's future earnings. At the same time, it denies the musician the one value for which he cares most of all: ownership of his songs.

While the above account is an accurate description of the Springsteen-Appel relationship, it is not a full or even a fair picture. Appel did get Bruce to sign a contract granting him a very high percentage of Bruce's earnings. He did this, he explained to the young musician, because he had heard it was the way that Elvis and the Colonel did things. This contract was later amended, but it was extremely greedy even for the record business. It never occurred to Springsteen to consult a lawyer or even to try to read the document himself. He merely carried the papers around in his pocket for a week and finally agreed to sign.

Still, the story is not quite the mercenary cliché it first appears. Appel's dedication to his client was nothing short of devotional. Bruce was a "religion" to Appel, and he considered himself its John the Baptist. He mortgaged his home and maxed out a succession of credit cards. Under Appel's care Bruce never heard about money and was never told that anything he needed was unreasonable or unaffordable. He simply informed Appel of what he thought he needed to pursue his muse, and Appel did his best to provide it.

Appel was a man obsessed. He passed one holiday season sending bags of coal wrapped in Christmas stockings to all the deejays he felt had scrimped on playing Bruce. Appel once called up an NBC television producer to suggest that his unknown client sing at the Super Bowl.

(Memories differ as to whether he wanted Bruce to sing "The Star-Spangled Banner" or, more implausibly, an antiwar original called "Balboa vs. The Earth Slayer.") When the producer responded that Andy Williams and Blood, Sweat and Tears were already booked, Appel reportedly yelled, "They're losers, and you're a loser, too. Someday I'm going to give you a call and remind you of this. Then I'm going to make another call, and you'll be out of a job." Yet another Appel story involves a late-night drive he took with Peter Philbin, a Columbia publicist and Springsteen devotee, before the release of Bruce's third album. Appel asked just how many copies Philbin expected the record to sell. When Philbin said between 500,000 and 800,000, somewhere between twenty-five and eighty times as many as either of Bruce's first two records had sold upon their initial releases, Appel pulled the car over to the curb and ordered the apostate onto the street. Screaming, "Get out of the car! Get out of the car!" Appel sped off into the night, horrified at Philbin's insufficient faith.

The word *legend* is tossed around nowhere so promiscuously as in the music industry, but it can hardly be avoided when introducing the subject of John Hammond. A Vanderbilt scion who covered the Scottsboro Boys' trial for *The Nation* magazine, Hammond built a career around his two lifelong passions: jazz and racial justice. He often managed to combine the two by promoting the careers of unknown artists of color and folksingers of uncommon vision and social commitment. During a career that spanned half a century, the tireless talent scout either discovered or played a key role in producing and promoting the careers of Bessie Smith, Billie Holiday, Alberta Hunter, Benny Goodman, Teddy Wilson, the Count Basie Orchestra, Lionel Hampton, Charlie Christian, Aretha Franklin, George Benson, Leonard Cohen, Stevie Ray Vaughan, Pete Seeger, and, yes, Bob Dylan.

One early spring day in 1972, Mike Appel escorted his skinny, hungry client to see the sixty-one-year-old patrician producer in his Columbia Records offices and announced, "So you're the guy who found Bob Dylan. I wanna see if that was just a fluke, or if you really have ears, because I've got somebody much better than him." Hammond quite reasonably replied, "For God's sake, just stop it! You're going to make me hate you." He could not have known that Springsteen was, at that moment, in the process of reading Anthony Scaduto's biography of Dylan, which, given Hammond's own role in that story, no doubt amplified the young man's mortification. Springsteen recalled that he "went into a state of shock as soon as [he] walked in. Before I ever played a note, Mike starts screamin' and yellin' 'bout me. I'm shrivelin' up and thinkin', 'Please, Mike, give me a break. Let me play a damn song.' So, dig this, before I ever played a note, the hype began." (Hammond, for the record, later described Appel, as "offensive as any man I've ever met" but "utterly selfless in his devotion to Bruce.")

That Bruce survived Appel's introduction is merely one of the amazing details of that fateful day. A second is that he chose to play "Mary Queen of Arkansas," almost certainly the most morose and pretentious song he has ever released.* Moreover, the talent scout had agreed to listen to the boy strictly on the hunch of his secretary, who had fielded Appel's first over-the-top entreaty. Hammond was intrigued enough by what he heard to cancel the rest of his calendar for the morning and listen to Springsteen play. Bruce, said Appel, left Hammond's office and "literally skipped down the street." Bruce remembered feeling "excited," for his "whole world was transformed" by the meeting with Hammond. "I'd written some good songs, and this was my shot."

Hammond arranged for Springsteen to play an early set at the Gaslight in Greenwich Village that night in front of about a dozen people. Bruce in his folksinger guise impressed Hammond with his ability to connect with the audience. The following day, May 3, 1972, Hammond arranged a demo recording at which Bruce recorded twelve songs, five of which would eventually make it onto *Greetings from Asbury Park*: "It's Hard to Be a Saint in the City," "Mary Queen of Arkansas," "Growin' Up," "Does This Bus Stop at 82nd Street?" and

* "Mary" was the runaway winner in the fanzine *Backstreets'* 1991 poll in the category of worst Springsteen song ever, besting its closest competition by a two-to-one margin. It also took the honors in a similar poll conducted by the Internet mailing list "LuckyTown Digest" in 1996.

"The Angel." Once again, it is a tribute to Hammond that he heard genius in songs that were, even by the standards of Springsteen's talent at the time, generally subpar. Of the twelve songs recorded that day, only "Growin' Up," "Saint in the City," and perhaps "Does This Bus" have stood the test of repeated listenings. "The Angel" actually rivals "Mary" in both pretense and ploddingness, and finished second in the *Backstreets* "worst ever" poll. The most interesting songs Bruce played that day, "If I Was the Priest," "Cowboys of the Sea," and "Arabian Nights," never made it onto any official Springsteen release.

Nevertheless, "the kid absolutely knocked me out," Hammond later said. "On the recording sheet, a log the company requires for all studio auditions, I wrote, 'Greatest talent of the decade,' or some such understatement." Hammond asked Appel to have a lawyer he trusted look at the two men's contract to make certain that everything was on the up-and-up for a Columbia signing. According to the Appel-CBS accord, Bruce would make a total of ten albums, and Appel's company, which he then owned with his partner, Jim Cretecos, would receive a lion's share of all profits. The lawyer called the Springsteen-Appel partnership deal "a slave contract" and promised Appel that "your artist — if he makes it — is going to hate you." Hammond said he tried to warn Bruce about this, but Bruce was too loyal to Appel to heed him.

Hammond signed Springsteen to Columbia within a month on June 9, 1972, to a contract in which the artist received a $25,000 advance against $65,000 in production costs for his first album. Bruce did not even have an address at the time. Appel, who had Springsteen signed simultaneously to concurrent management, production, and music-publishing agreements, took the money but was not even professional enough to open a business account separate from his own personal accounts. Just under 50 percent of the initial advance went into setting up Appel's spiffy new offices in the same Midtown building as Dylan's manager, Albert Grossman. (Springsteen, meanwhile, was crashing in a sleeping bag on a friend's floor.) Little more than $10,000 was spent on the task of recording Bruce Springsteen's first album.

The recording itself took place in late June at 914 Studios in Blauvelt, New York, quite a distance from the Jersey dives where Bruce and the other musicians were crashing but where a friend of Appel's offered unlimited recording time and unlimited credit. Hammond had planned to be on hand to lend some guidance to the two studio novices. But Appel scheduled the sessions to begin at midnight, and Hammond, who was recovering from a third heart attack, was under doctor's orders to go to bed early. He suspected that Appel had chosen so late a time on purpose, since Hammond had wanted to record Springsteen with just a guitar, as he had initially recorded Dylan. Springsteen remembered that Appel and Cretecos "were always very production-oriented: they were big Cat Stevens fans at the time, and he had these very enhanced acoustic records." Springsteen himself also wanted a rhythm section and a band, and fearing that an acoustic album would die on the radio, CBS president Clive Davis concurred. So Appel and Bruce went off to make a rock 'n' roll record, though neither had a terribly clear idea of how rock 'n' roll records got made.

The result was something of an unholy mess — an acoustic album with a band and rhythm section, cheaply recorded with a reconstituted but underrehearsed Bruce Springsteen Band. As Gary Tallent later observed, "We had no experience in the studio whatsoever before that first record and, at times, it showed." There were no adults in the studio to ensure any kind of professional discipline, and Springsteen could not control the avalanche of poetic verbiage that he was then employing as song lyrics. ("Wizard imps and sweat-sock pimps, interstellar mongrel nymphs.") "I let out an incredible number of things at once," Springsteen said of that group of songs, "a million things in each song. They were written in half-hour, fifteen-minute bursts. I don't know where they came from. A few of them I worked on for a week or so, but most of them were just jets."

We may judge the power of the lightning storm of creativity surging through young Bruce Springsteen by the fact that the record's most distinctive songs, "Blinded by the Light" and "Spirit in the Night," were written after the initial recording was finished, when Clive Davis complained of its lack of singles. They are both great songs, but they are not singles. Each line in "Blinded by the Light" includes three rhyming words and a fourth that rhymes with the end of the subsequent phrase, twenty syllables per line. The mere opening of the song, "Madman drummers, bummers and Indians in the summer with a teenage diplomat / In the dumps with the mumps as the adolescent pumps his way into his hat," announces that it is hardly radio-friendly. And in order to complete the recording of "Spirit," Springsteen decided he had to locate the sax player he had known in Asbury Park, Clarence Clemons. But the big black sax man had no known address, and no one knew how to find him. Recording was delayed, therefore, until a change was made uptown and the Big Man joined the band.

Recorded in just three weeks, with the main tracks laid down in just seven days, *Greetings* has its moments of power and romance. "Spirit in the Night" is a magical character-driven evocation of friendship, romance, and adventure and a can't-get-it-out-of-your mind, horn-driven melody. "Growin' Up," "For You," "Saint in the City," and "Lost in the Flood" also serve to announce the arrival of a poet of considerable reach and ambition. Each manages to combine elements of Springsteen's volatile talents into a (just) manageable mix. One moment he is an ironic teenage troubadour who "hid in the clouded wrath of the crowd but when they said, 'Sit down,' I stood up." On another, he is all adolescent braggadocio, the "king of the alley . . . prince of the paupers . . . the pimp's main prophet" who made even "the sisters [fall] back and [say,] 'Don't that man look pretty.'" On yet another, he is the wounded ex-lover of a disturbed girl who "did not need [his] urgency," owing to the fact that her "life was one long emergency," and now "[her] cloud line urges me and my electric surges free." It's hard to know just what Bruce is saying, but as the old song goes, "he was really saying something."

Timothy White smartly termed the album's songwriter "a dialogue-starved young parkway philosopher who could not hold back his observations on the suburban curbside buffet." Most of the lyrics, Bruce has noted, are "twisted autobiographies" that "found their seed in people, places, hangouts, and incidents" he had seen and the things he had lived. Bruce said he "wrote impressionistically and changed names to protect the guilty." Both "the lyrics and spirit of *Greetings* came from a very unself-conscious place . . . a moment when [I was] writing with no prospect of ever being heard." Looking back, Bruce remembered working "to find something that was identifiably mine."

Unfortunately, the sound that Bruce considered identifiably his was also viewed, both at Columbia and throughout much of the industry, as identifiably Bob Dylan's. It did not help that Bruce's scraggly hair and scruffy dark beard gave him an uncanny resemblance to the Bard of Hibbing, who was then at the height of one of his post–motorcycle accident/silenced oracle phases. The music business had created categories into which all new acts were necessarily shoehorned. Columbia president Clive Davis, a big Bruce-booster, noted quite accurately at the time that "the challenge to the company is how to deal with someone who is gifted with thorough originality and is special. And in this day and age, where so many articles and company statements are being made about various artists, they all tended to merge after a while. That's why everybody runs into a problem when something extra-special rather than special comes along. How do you do it in a manner which is tasteful and which is true to your artist's integrity?"

It was a tough test, and despite Davis's best intentions, Columbia failed. For marketing purposes, the young rocker was not only pigeonholed into the ill-fitting "singer-songwriter" bracket but was also confined to the artistic straitjacket of being the newest of the "new Dylans" (where he was eventually joined by Loudon Wainwright III, John Prine, Elliott Murphy, and Steve Forbert, among others). This tag would prove burdensome. In the first place, Dylan's mythology at that moment was so great that no mere mortal — including Bob Dylan — could possibly have made an album sufficiently poetic and original to live up to it (at least not until 1975's *Blood on the Tracks*). Second, while Springsteen did confess to loving *Highway 61 Revisited* as a teenager, it was only one of a multitude of influences on his still-unformed musical identity. It was, he recalled, "a map," but he followed his own road. Columbia, Bruce complained, "forgot about the eight years [of rock 'n' roll bands] and went with the two months [of solo performing]." That is, they went with Dylan and forgot about Elvis — to say nothing of James Brown.

The album tanked so completely and the singles disappeared so quickly that, in the case of "Spirit in the Night," no one alive has ever credibly claimed to have seen one. Springsteen was booked as the warm-up for an arena tour by the band Chicago, which proved a catastrophe. He also gave an unfortunate performance before a CBS convention, at which he impressed people with nothing so much as the apparent chip on his shoulder. Both reduced his professional stock even further. Hammond was horrified, and Davis deeply disappointed. But Springsteen kept plugging. "With a record contract and a touring band, I was better off than most of my friends," he remembered thinking. "They were either jobless or locked down into the nine-to-five. I felt lucky to be doing what I loved most." And his work was not *entirely* ignored. *Stereo Review* picked the album as one of the year's ten best. Its reviewer, Steve Simels, called the music "absolutely haunting" and the band "fantastic," noting that the album "reminds me of what Van Morrison might be doing if he ever stopped whining." Simels bemoaned the "kiss-of-death 'new Dylan' hype," however, and promised his readers that "despite the fact that most of the current crop of singer-songwriters give me a swift pain, I have no doubt that this kid's really got it."

In July 1973, the "kid" was back in Blauvelt, working to erase the "new Dylan" stigma with a new album.

The Wild, the Innocent & the E Street Shuffle was re-corded under the same penny-wise, pound-foolish cir-cumstances as *Greetings*, though Springsteen appears to have had a clearer idea of where he wanted to take his music. Once again the album was recorded on the fly, in less than two months of sporadic studio time.

Despite the limitations of its production values, *Wild & Innocent* emerged an inconsistent masterpiece. It is driven lyrically by the ideals of postadolescent life on the Jersey Shore: the notion of a loose community of al-most adults brought together by music, romance, and re-lief from the pressures of all forms of authority. The lyrics never leave New Jersey, except on imagined excur-sions across the river. (Springsteen would introduce "New York City Serenade" in concert by proclaiming, "I been to Manhattan a lot lately, and this is how it shoulda been.") With the album's emphasis on "placeness," Springsteen's Asbury Park serves the same purpose as Joyce's Dublin or Roth's Newark. The zoom-lens focus helps make the particular universal and vice versa.

Musically, the album is an adventurous amalgam of styles. "We were folk musicians," Bruce recalled. "Peo-ple played very personally and very eccentrically," not unlike a carnival band. The album is heavy with San-cious's jazz piano and Danny Federici's haunting accor-dion. Timothy White once again caught its emotional atmosphere when he termed it "almost a vociferous afterthought smoothing out the contradictions of the first record." On *Wild & Innocent* he heard "an impatient, suddenly lucid romantic who had stayed up all night . . . an impulsive visionary with plenty of time to kill." Again, with few cuts shorter than seven minutes, nothing on the album remotely resembled a hit single.

The introductory track, "The E Street Shuffle," Bruce noted, reflects "a community that was partly imagined and partly real." It is based on the kind of blues, R&B, and soul still popular on the Jersey Shore, particularly a sixties hit by Major Lance called "The Monkey Time." The characters are vaguely based on Jersey Shore musicians. Bruce wanted to describe "a neighborhood, a way of life" and hoped to "invent a dance with no exact steps." Just before embarking on the album, Springsteen had been kicked out of the beauty-parlor rooms in Asbury Park and had moved into a garage apartment with his then girlfriend in Bradley Beach, five miles down the road. "4th of July, Asbury Park (Sandy)" serves as a farewell to Springsteen's adopted hometown of Asbury Park and the life he lived there. (Sandy, for the record, is a composite of girls Bruce had known along the Shore.) The closing-down of the town and the end of summer romance — the cops' shutting down of Madame Marie's "for tellin' fortunes better than they do" — are transformed into a metaphor for the end of adolescence. The album's highlights, "Rosalita" and "Kitty's Back," are Springsteen's self-conscious efforts to write big. He wanted to create music that would grab people's attention even though it was being performed in a smoky bar where the band would not normally be the focus of attention. These showstoppers were designed to leave the audience exhausted and gasping for breath.

"Rosalita," in particular, is a rock 'n' roll milestone. An ecstatic seven-minute warhorse of a song, it would close virtually every Springsteen performance for the next eleven years. It is the kind of song — like "Louie, Louie" or "I Saw Her Standing There" — that is at the top of a pile of records one holds in reserve for the proverbial Martian who comes to Earth and asks, "Just what *is* this rock 'n' roll stuff, anyway?" Springsteen viewed the song — embodying all the great themes of love, rebellion, friendship, escape, and adventure — as his "musical autobiography" and "a kiss-off to everybody who counted you out, put you down, or decided you weren't good enough." When Rosalita's father objects to her new raffish boyfriend, she is advised: "Tell him this is his last chance to get his daughter in a fine romance / Because the record company, Rosie, just gave me a big advance!"

Wild & Innocent failed no less rapidly than *Greetings*. Part of the blame lay in Springsteen's unwillingness — in a fit of "quit comparing me to Dylan" pique — to print the lyrics to the songs on the album sleeve. (To this day, it is impossible to make out the words that begin "Kitty's Back.") Moreover, if Springsteen wasn't the new Dylan, or even the new James Taylor, then just what *was* he? In 1974 the country was mired in the muck of the sixties and its unpleasant aftermath. Nixon was dragging the end of his presidency out interminably, and Kissinger was doing the same with Vietnam. By far the biggest musical event of the year was Dylan's decision to reunite with the Band for an album and a national tour. They earned a great deal of money but added little to either's artistic legacy. Nonsense like Ray Stevens's "The Streak" ruled the AM radio dial, while on FM, program directors were enraptured by the pretensions of "progressive rock" bands like Yes or the Moody Blues on the one hand and the androgynous antics of "glam-rock" stars like David Bowie or Marc Bolan of T-Rex on the other. Rock's brief history and radio stations' narrowly defined playlists could find no precedent for an artist who combined folk with blues with jazz with R&B with soul with guitar-driven, Latin-tinged beats — all in the service of dizzying cascades of street poetry. *Wild & Innocent* earned considerable critical praise but sold barely more than its predecessor, thereby endangering the possibility of even allowing Bruce a third strike. When Clive Davis, who had always taken a special interest in Springsteen, was forced out of the top job at Columbia, Bruce could hardly be blamed if he feared for his future.

What saved Springsteen from professional oblivion during this period was the same thing that had earned him his place originally: his almost mystical relationship to the secret language of rock 'n' roll. It's hard to imagine, but the same Bruce Springsteen who could not get arrested on a sales chart may already have developed into the music's greatest performer.

As early as March 1973, *Crawdaddy*'s Peter Knobler saw the twenty-three-year-old Bruce Springsteen in a solo set and was immediately knocked out. He wrote an enthusiastic article titled "Who Is Bruce Springsteen and Why Are We Saying All These Wonderful Things About Him." Springsteen didn't even mind that *Crawdaddy* referred to him as "the heralded Bruce Springstein." "Hey, lookit," he told Knobler. "I'm heralded!"

Springsteen's performing legend grew in strange fits and starts. In some towns he looked like a superstar. In others almost as many people were on the stage as in the audience. At one January 1973 concert at Villanova University, his concert sold only twenty-five tickets. Three months later the band backed up Chuck Berry at a gig, but Chuck showed up late and neglected to tell them what songs he was playing. Bruce's road earnings rose from $2,250 in 1972 to $41,000 in 1973, of which Bruce's take was $5,000. By these standards 1974 was a banner year: everyone in the band, including Bruce, earned $8,500 before taxes. When they toured in the South, Vini Lopez would sometimes fish for the band's dinner. (Clarence's father had a fish market in Norfolk, and he was an expert fish trimmer.) Oftentimes the band would have to ask the audience if they could crash on their couches. In Boston one night, five band members slept on four mattresses in someone' attic. In Feburary 1974 Vini Lopez departed because of both artistic and personal problems. Sancious left to form his own band, and took Lopez's replacement, Ernest "Boom" Carter, with him.

Roy Bittan and Max Weinberg replaced them, respectively. When Miami Steve rejoined the band full-time, the lineup looked remarkably like the nucleus of Steel Mill, Dr. Zoom, and the Bruce Springsteen Band. Everyone was paid the same amount, which rose from $35 a week in 1973 to $350 in 1975. They were, as credibly as anyone could claim, not in it for the money. As John Hammond noted at the time, "In all my years of the business, [Bruce] is the only person who cares nothing about money."

Together, Bruce Springsteen and the E Street Band, as they were called beginning in late 1972, had begun to play music that left people voiceless, speechless, or both. Some performers who made the mistake of allowing Springsteen to open their concerts, like Anne Murray in Central Park during August of 1974, never got a chance to sing. Smarter, savvier headliners, like John Sebastian, simply asked if they could warm up the warm-up, after watching the band run through its sound check.

In person Bruce was still painfully shy. These were the days when he would ride the bus to the offices of *Crawdaddy* magazine off of lower Fifth Avenue to hang out with its editors, Peter Knobler and Greg Mitchell. But with his craggy looks and lumpen proletariat dress, Springsteen was rarely able to make it past the building's receptionist, who took him for a bicycle messenger. Unwilling to correct this misimpression himself, Springsteen would just stand idly in the waiting area until someone on the staff finally recognized him. Springsteen also went to Yankee games with the staff, the editors would recall, without saying a word for the entire nine innings.

But Bruce Springsteen the performer was someone else entirely. One of Appel's coworkers told an interviewer, "When Bruce got on a stage, Mike and I would sit there and say, 'Where are all these stories coming from?' Bruce didn't just get onstage and kick ass. Bruce got onstage and was funny. He'd introduce a song for five minutes. People would roll in the aisles, and then he'd play the song. That was all intact when we met him. Bruce had his persona; he knew what he wanted to do." Bruce could be the charming innocent, as when he told an audience of six hundred people a story in which he got into some trouble with the New Jersey Mafia and added, "Now hey, that's in confidence. I wouldn't want that to go outside this room." He could poke fun at himself, describing a terrible trip to Mexico his family made by noting, "As usual, I was able to shrug off the reality of the situation and romanticize myself into writing a tune about it."

But most of all, it was the music. Springsteen was so prolific during this period that he was writing classic rock 'n' roll that he would not find a way to release for more than twenty-five years, when it would still sound fresh. "Thundercrack," which would not appear until 1998, would, like "Rosalita" and "Kitty's Back," drive crowds crazy. "The Fever," which Springsteen finally emancipated in 1999, would put virtually the entire audience into a kind of trance. (David Sancious had been under the impression it was an old Sam Cooke classic.) Springsteen also took obscure old songs that few people remembered and shook them back into life. The Crystals' "And Then [S]he Kissed Me," the Searchers' "When You Walk in the Room," and most particularly, Gary "U.S." Bonds's "Quarter to Three" roused crowds as they had probably never done before. These were not "oldies," in Bruce's view, for as he explained, "They may be older songs . . . but they are great right now." As he told an interviewer in 1974, beginning in 1967 he owned no record player, and his girlfriend only had an "old beat-up one that only old records sounded good on." So he had absorbed these songs as if they were still ruling the airwaves, and played them with the same urgency. By seamlessly incorporating these forgotten historical treasures into his repertoire, Springsteen gave further stimulus to the quietly growing critical belief that he was somehow channeling the pure spirit of rock 'n' roll. Peter Knobler compared the experience of seeing Bruce for the first time to being ushered "into the Big Pink in 1967 [if] you'd never heard of Dylan." But it was Jon Landau, perhaps the most influential critic writing at the time, who saw in Bruce Springsteen the possibility of a performer who could rescue rock music from the depths into which it had fallen and perhaps even begin to reconstruct the culture as well. It was May 9, 1974, and Springsteen was playing a small theater in Cambridge, Massachusetts, where Landau lived. Bruce's show was a typical one in most respects, except that he had debuted a new song he had yet to record, called "Born to Run."

At the time, Landau's marriage was falling apart, his health was collapsing, and his faith in the music that had sustained him through other difficult periods of his life was teetering on the brink. Landau discovered in a single Bruce Springsteen show everything that had ever excited him about rock 'n' roll in the first place. And he said so in a voice so personal, so knowledgeable, and so compelling that it turned Bruce's record company around and convinced it that it was sitting not on a guy with nearly invisible sales figures but on "rock & roll's future." Ironically, the famous phrase, soon blazoned across countless full-page advertisements purchased by Columbia, was almost perfectly misleading. Not much of rock 'n' roll's future could be found in Bruce Springsteen's music: not techno, not funk, not punk, not disco, not acid-house, not rap. What it did contain, however, was a convincing distillation of what had made rock 'n' roll so exciting in the past. As Bob Dylan would observe more than a decade later, "Bruce knows where he comes from — he has taken what everybody else has done and made his own thing of it." Landau described the performer as "dressed like a reject from Sha Na Na . . . [parading] in front of his all-star rhythm band like a cross between Chuck Berry, early Bob Dylan, and Marlon Brando." And it was these elements of Springsteen's musical persona that he forged into something that was as old as it was new. But it was also "real" in a way that the critic had almost given up on ever encountering again. Despite his considerable eloquence, Landau ultimately found himself at a loss for words. In trying to describe something that could only be seen, heard, felt, and ultimately experienced, he finally fell back on the old Lovin' Spoonful lyric: he would tell us about the magic that would free our souls, "but it was like trying to tell a stranger about rock and roll."

Well the change was made uptown

    and the Big Man joined the band

From the coastline to the city

    all the little pretties raised a hand

— "Tenth Avenue Freeze-Out," 1975

Tramps Like Us ...

Following the commercial failure of both *Greetings* and *Wild & Innocent*, the disastrous 1974 tour opening for Chicago, and the departure of Clive Davis from CBS, Springsteen's future at Columbia hung by a slender thread indeed. Springsteen himself felt the chill of the changed atmosphere at Columbia but was powerless to affect it. He bought himself a brief reprieve when, after playing a gig at Brown University, a student journalist interviewed him, and Bruce mentioned his freeze-out at the record company, blaming it on the company's new president, Irwin Segelstein. Segelstein happened to have a son at Brown, and the young man and his friends were all Springsteen fanatics. The kid saw the interview in the student newspaper, called his dad, and complained. Segelstein decided to take another look at the young man with the great reviews and the paltry sales.

Jon Landau's *Real Paper* review, appearing at exactly

the right moment, transformed the manner in which Springsteen was perceived at the record label. In receiving the most enthusiastic accolades imaginable from perhaps the most influential rock critic alive, Springsteen was no longer under pressure merely to make a profit; now he had to be a prophet. After two perceived strikes, he was now expected to step up to the proverbial plate and hit a Babe Ruth–size home run all the way from Yankee Stadium to the lions' cages in the Bronx Zoo. Springsteen did not exactly relish the challenge, but neither did he shrink from it. Having learned from his mistakes, he was ready, he thought, to make "the greatest rock 'n' roll record of all time" — or at least to kill himself trying.

The record Bruce had in mind would "explode in people's homes and minds and change people's lives." It would be an album with a "sound like Phil Spector . . . words like Dylan . . . [and guitars] like Duane Eddy," something that, obviously, none of them could have hoped to achieve themselves. During the past year Bruce had been listening primarily to Roy Orbison, the Ronettes, and the Beach Boys. He wanted them in there, too. This time he was not going to let go of the master tapes until they matched the sound in his head.

Just how all these tasks might be accomplished simultaneously, however, was a question with almost unlimited answers, and Bruce seemed to want to explore each one in detail. After six months of nonstop recording, the band had completed exactly one song; good thing it was "Born to Run."

To try to keep Columbia's interest from flagging and the faithful from forgetting, Appel had been sneaking bootleg tapes of unreleased songs to sympathetic deejays. A slow, mournful version of "The Fever" filled the airwaves in Philadelphia, Cleveland, Austin, and Phoenix until it was replaced by "Born to Run" a few months later. This amazing song, which ultimately showcases approximately a dozen guitar tracks, a massive sax solo, a glockenspiel, a fancy string arrangement, and numerous keyboard tracks, along with the requisite bass guitar and drums, created a considerable commotion wherever it was heard, whether on the radio or in concert. On WMMS in Cleveland, the deejay Kid Leo played it at 5:55 every Friday. Record-store clerks were driven crazy by Springsteen fans trying to find it. How in the world, the Columbia executives asked themselves, have we found ourselves in the position of having signed the Future of Rock 'n' Roll, who after three years has produced only two albums that won't sell and a monster hit he won't release?

Springsteen's debts to the company were piling up as the recording of "Born to Run" continued interminably. Yet Bruce would not be moved. With remarkable self-possession for an artist in his precarious professional position he insisted, as he told rock journalist Paul Nelson during the sessions, "When it's ready, it'll be there. . . . I decided a long time ago; I know who I am and where I come from. And I know what it is to be caught up in the pressure. You start thinking that you're something else. You start becoming a product of the entertainment business. I try to keep my perspective on the thing. It's even for the good of the record company that I do that, because I'll give 'em my best and it'll work out for the best in the end."

So back into the studio he went. Over Appel's vociferous objection, Bruce invited his new friend Jon Landau, who had produced undistinguished albums for the MC5 and Livingston Taylor, to join the production team in February 1975, and the now ex-critic managed to wring some progress from the proceedings. Perhaps most important, he convinced Springsteen to move from Blauvelt to the more expensive Record Plant in Times Square, where at least the pedal on the piano would not be audible in the sound mix. Before Landau arrived, Springsteen said he did not even know he was "screwing up." Yes, the record "sounded like a bunch of noise," but he was under the impression that everything was going "like diamonds."

Another breakthrough occurred the night old friend and fellow rock 'n' roll itinerant Steve Van Zandt came by the studio to visit. No one had been able to figure out how to make the horn section of "Tenth Avenue Freeze-Out" work, until Steve asked if he could give it a try. He sang their parts to each of the players; the sound worked perfectly, and he was back in the band. But even with

Landau's welcome contributions and Van Zandt's inspiring presence, progress remained slow and tempers fierce. A single recording session might last twenty-four hours, with Springsteen drifting between studios, singing "She's the One" in one room, mixing "Jungleland" in another studio downstairs, and rehearsing the band for a live performance in a third.

"The album became a monster," he complained. "It wanted everything. It just ate up everyone's life." His own perfectionism, Bruce later noted, "was wrecking me, just pounding me into the ground." It didn't help matters that Springsteen was staying at a run-down hotel in Times Square, living in "like the worst room in the world . . . with the whores and prostitutes knocking at my door every night." Each day he had to leave his girlfriend, who had come in from Texas and didn't know anyone in New York, at the room all alone. His nerves started to go, and his behavior veered a bit off-kilter. For example, Springsteen grew obsessed with the motel room's mirror: "The mirror was crooked. That sucker was as crooked as crooked could be; it just hung crooked. Couldn't get it to hang right. It just blew my mind after a certain amount of time. . . It was the album that mirror became — it was crooked, it just wouldn't hang right." To top it all off, just as the company's absolutely final deadline was approaching, Springsteen decided he hated everything he had completed so far. "It was the worst piece of garbage I'd ever heard," he remembered thinking. "We walked out of that studio, and I wanted to kill somebody." He even tried to tell Columbia that he would refuse to release it. They could record him at the Bottom Line playing his new songs, if they wanted, and release that instead.

Imagine: Bruce Springsteen wanted to throw out *Born to Run*. He wanted to junk the album that Lester Bangs insisted "reminds us what it's like to love rock 'n' roll like you just discovered it," that Greil Marcus considered "a magnificent album that pays off on every bet ever placed on him — a '57 Chevy running on melted-down Crystals records that shuts down every claim that has been made," that Pete Townshend deemed a "fucking triumph." Thank God Springsteen had, in Jon Landau, someone who could say to him: "Look, you're not supposed to like it. You think Chuck Berry sits around listening to 'Maybellene'? And when he does hear it, don't you think that he wishes a few things could be changed? Now come on, it's time to put the record out." On July 20, 1975, Springsteen finally surrendered the acetates.

If ever any rock 'n' roll record can be said to have been needed in a certain time and place, then *Born to Run* is the record, and America 1975 is the time and place. Recall the cultural atmosphere of the country in the mid-seventies. Pretty much everything that had given sixties culture its passion, energy, and creativity had disappeared and been replaced by exhaustion and exploitation. The revolution was over. Apart from a few small pockets of resistance, most rock music had become robotic and repetitive when it was not self-parodic. As

Peter Guralnick wrote back in 1971: "What for us was a liberating act . . . has become . . . something a great deal more serious and infinitely less important." The decade began with three major rock icons destroying themselves in fits of self-indulgent excess. Bobby, Martin, and John may have died as a symbol of a nation at war with itself, but Jimi, Janis, and Jim Morrison died for no one's sins but their own.

Viewed in the context of the impractical dreams of erstwhile sixties revolutionaries and flower children, the seventies take on a certain kind of historical inevitability. A nation on the cusp of revolution and, potentially, repressive reaction, fighting a corrupt war under corrupt leadership, is entitled to a bout of frivolousness once it's all over. But to those of us who came of age during this period, with more than a whiff of enthusiasm, idealism, energy, and desire to remake the world — or at least the circumstances of our own lives — it was a singularly hellish time to be young.

Inside post-Watergate, post-Vietnam, post-idealism America, the economic foundations of prosperity were under siege. Following the 1973 Yom Kippur War, gasoline prices rose nearly 400 percent almost overnight. More than ten thousand gasoline stations went out of business that year, taking a whole way of life with them. In 1974 alone, retail prices increased by 11 percent and wholesale prices by 18 percent. The Dow Jones industrial average plunged 45 percent in less than two years. The recession seemed endless, and hope for a better future, pointless. By mid-1975, unemployment reached its highest point since the Depression as real GNP continued its apparently inexorable decline.

The effect of these economic shocks was particularly acute in the Northeast and Midwest, as skyrocketing oil prices and the loss of much of the U.S. manufacturing base shifted both power and population to the Southwest. Some 100,000 autoworkers lost their jobs in Detroit alone, depriving much of the small manufacturing and support economies of their lifeline as well. As the population followed hope for the future in a *Grapes of Wrath*–like caravan southwest, what were once thriving working-class neighborhoods began to feel like ghost towns. One newspaper headline during this period seemed to capture the national mood especially well: THINGS WILL GET WORSE BEFORE THEY GET WORSE.

Mainstream American culture in 1975 responded to this morass by seeking refuge in a kind of voluntary collective lobotomy. Among the period's most significant cultural icons were pet rocks, mood rings, coke spoons, and leisure suits; "It's no mai job, man," "Dyn-o-mite!" "Up your nose with a rubber hose," "Whip Inflation Now," and "Disco sucks" were the catchphrases of the day. In 1998 Rhino Records released a seven-CD set of the best of seventies pop music titled *Have a Nice Decade.* Contributions from 1975 include the Captain and Tennille's "Love Will Keep Us Together," Morris Albert's "Feelings," C. W. McCall's "Convoy," the Bay City Rollers' "Saturday Night," and, tellingly, the theme from the retro TV show *Happy Days.*

The celebration of superficiality represented just one aspect of the period's cultural personality. The other was a kind of public sadism, embodied by the public worship of self-conscious exclusivity. The height of this phenomenon was manifested by the glorification of the thuggish bouncers outside clubs like Studio 54 and Xenon, who mocked the pathetic ambitions of the suburbanites waiting on the street for the privilege of doing their lines in the bathroom alongside Mick or Liza. Discos perfected not only the velvet rope but also the VIP area, where the Truly Blessed were walled off from those expected to pay cash.

Idealism, in seventies culture, was treated as a kind of willful delusion. Consider the fates of the idealists in Scorsese's *Taxi Driver,* Coppola's *Godfather* films, Polanski's *Chinatown,* and Bogdanovich's *The Last Picture Show.* Is there a single moment on the Stones' masterpiece *Exile on Main Street* when a fan can unironically throw his fist in the air? Think of the difference between Sly Stone's "Stand!" or "I Want to Take You Higher" and his drug-addled, almost comatose *There's a Riot Goin' On.* In 1967 rock's avatars, the Beatles, invited us to "Sergeant Pepper's Lonely Hearts Club Band," and they hoped we would "enjoy the show." Nine years later we were gathered in the "master's chambers" of the Hotel California, where the music's new kings, the Eagles, were stabbing something "with their steely knives," but they just could not "kill the beast."

Having finally completed the ordeal of recording *Born to Run*, Bruce Springsteen and the newly reconstituted E Street Band arrived in New York for a ten-show stand at the Bottom Line during the third muggy week of August, as the city teetered on the edge of bankruptcy. Columbia's executives, by now well aware of the rough diamond in their midst, purchased nearly a quarter of all the tickets to distribute not only to media opinion makers but also to their own employees, to let them in on the secret. With its massive ticket purchase, "Future of Rock & Roll" publicity campaign, and $250,000 media buy, Columbia placed a bet on the relatively unknown Springsteen that was so big, no one could remember anything like it. It practically begged for a critical backlash. The Bottom Line shows therefore had the feeling of a kind of heavyweight championship fight, with Kid Springsteen up against the ghosts of the overhyped and undertalented contenders of media campaigns past.

Triumph was hardly a certainty. Springsteen had suffered a profound loss when keyboard player David Sancious — who was not only the band's most accomplished musician but also so integral to the formation of the band that it was named after the street where he lived — left with his friend "Boom" Carter. Alas, Bruce could not blame them. The entire band, including

Springsteen himself, was living on starvation wages. Columbia wanted Springsteen to hire studio musicians. Springsteen would not even consider this route, regardless of the delays replacements would create. "I don't hire studio musicians," he insisted. "I don't want guys with big houses playing for me. I just put an ad in the paper, and people come out and play. You take a kid off the street, and he'll play his heart out for you. If someone's primarily interested in how much money he's going to make, I don't want him playing for me."

That decision would prove its own wisdom many times over in future years. An ad was placed in the *Village Voice:* "Drummer (no jr. Ginger Bakers, must encompass R&B and jazz), pianist (classical to Jerry Lee Lewis), trumpet (must play r&b, Latin & jazz), violinist. All must sing. Male or female." Among the respondents keyboard player "Professor" Roy Bittan and drummer "Mighty" Max Weinberg auditioned for their respective parts. Each seemed to understand intuitively what was necessary to slip into what was about to become the ne plus ultra of rock 'n' roll bar bands. Danny Federici and Garry Tallent had played alongside Bruce since the Upstage days. The "Big Man," Clarence Clemons, on sax not only huffed and puffed like the son of King Curtis but also provided the perfect dramatic foil for the scrawny little guy with the mike onstage. The band, as a unit, worked at fever pitch. "We knew what we wanted, and we knew we were good," recalled Clemons. "And this was our chance to shine, to show the world we were ready."

The casual racial mixture of the band — despite the loss of two black members — also helped give it a kind of utopian gloss of musical male camaraderie. And with the return of Bruce's oldest and closest friend, guitarist Steve Van Zandt, into the fold, it found its collective heart and soul just in time to bare them before the world. The sum of the parts became a medium channeling the pure, rebellious, celebratory spirit of the music into a mighty whole: the "close band of merry thieves" of rock 'n' roll yore with a nod toward the not-quite-forgotten dreams of the "We Shall Overcome" period of optimistic American liberalism.

The response to the Bottom Line shows was everything Columbia could have wished for — and more, no doubt, than young Bruce could ever have imagined. On a purely musical level Bruce was so elated that he finished the sets jumping up and down like a prizefighter punching the air with both hands. "The band cruised through them shows like the finest machine there was," he said. "There's nothin' — nothin' — in the world to get you playing better than a gig like that." As for the critics, they responded as if they were seeing a real-life rock 'n' roll fairy tale coming true before their eyes. As Peter Knobler admitted in *Crawdaddy:* "I had become accustomed to lackluster rock 'n' roll, had lowered the standards for a good time. What had become tolerable became good; what had felt good before became, through lack of anything better, great. It was love the one you're with or live without love. So when Bruce stepped on-stage, I had forgotten what it was all about. Lucky me."

Knobler was only one of a chorus of formerly cynical critics who rediscovered the joys of their youth and punched out words on their typewriters that they had never expected to see again. John Rockwell cried, "Springsteen's entrances were greeted with standing ovations, and by the end of each set, the crowd's mood was one of delirium"; Dave Marsh, a protégé of Landau's who would soon become Springsteen's Boswell, crowed, "Springsteen is everything that has been claimed for him — a magical guitarist, singer, writer, rock 'n' roll re-juvenator. He is the living culmination of twenty years of rock tradition." Ken Tucker proclaimed, "I have just come from the best rock 'n' roll performance I've seen in my long, decadent life. Springsteen may well be the sav-ior of rock 'n' roll." WNEW-FM deejay Dave Herman, who refused to even play Springsteen's first album be-cause of what he then suspected as hype, actually apolo-gized to his audience on the air. "I saw Springsteen for the first time last night," he explained. "It was the most exciting rock 'n' roll show I've ever seen."

These reviews, moreover, were replicated all across the country as the band set out on tour. And Spring-steen's own insistence on performing in small halls and clubs only ratcheted up the hysteria. After seeing him rock the Roxy as he had the Bottom Line, Robert Hill-burn of the *Los Angeles Times* called Springsteen "the purest glimpse of the passion and power of rock 'n' roll in nearly a decade." A writer from *Playboy* wondered if the entire audience was on Springsteen's payroll.

With an initial press run of only 175,000 copies, *Born to Run* received orders of 350,000 and sold 700,000 copies in its first two months, on its way to becoming rock music's first certified million-selling "platinum" record. For the first time in the history of entertainment journalism, both *Time* and *Newsweek* agreed to Mike Appel's "no cover, no interview" conditions and put Bruce on their covers during the same week. Annoyed, perhaps, by the way Appel had manipulated it when the star could barely bring himself to sit down for an interview, *Newsweek* began the inevitable backlash, publishing a piece that focused less on the artist than on the hype surrounding him. *Time,* on the other hand, played it relatively straight, calling Bruce "a glorified gutter rat from a dying New Jersey resort town who walks with an easy swagger that is part residual stage presence, part boardwalk braggadocio." Still, *Time*'s Jay Cocks understood as few before him that while Bruce had many influences, he was not the "new" anyone. "Springsteen's songs," he wrote, "are full of echoes — of Sam Cooke and Elvis Presley, of Chuck Berry, Roy Orbison and Buddy Holly. You can also hear Bob Dylan, Van Morrison and the Band weaving among Springsteen's elaborate fantasias." Neither magazine could avoid pointing out just how great he was at making rock 'n' roll. Cocks wrote: "He is neither sentimental nor superficial. His music is primal, directly in touch with all the impulses of wild humor and glancing melancholy, street tragedy and punk anarchy that have made rock the distinctive voice of a generation."

It was my voice, too. In the summer of 1975 I was thoroughly miserable. I was always in trouble at school, with teachers and coaches, and could not get along with any member of my family. My career as a jock was coming to a rapid close, and I seemed to be replacing it with pot, poker, and petty larceny. I was bored and unmoored. I loved rock 'n' roll, but I hated what I heard on the radio.

At fifteen, I was still three years away from being legally allowed into the Bottom Line, where alcohol was served, and my brand-new New York State Official ID Card, purchased for $3.50 in Times Square for exactly this purpose, failed to convince. Fortunately, WNEW-FM broadcast the August 15 show on the radio. I, too, was betting on Bruce to deliver something I could never have defined. I remember walking around the city that summer, seeing Springsteen on posters hung up on the side of Dumpsters and abandoned construction sites. I bought the first two albums and waited impatiently.

And somehow Springsteen delivered. The collective delirium poured out of my little boom box that night, and I shouted into the sky, "Tramps, like us, baby, we were borrrrraaaaaaaarrrrrrn!" lying on the football field outside my high school on the night of the broadcast, drinking little Miller eight-packs with my best friend. *Born to Run* exploded in my home and my mind and changed my life, just as Elvis and the Beatles had done for Bruce a decade earlier. I could never have articulated it at the time, but *Born to Run* offered me an alternative context for my life, a narrative in which hopes and dreams that felt ridiculous were accorded dignity and, no less important, solidarity.

What made this music so powerful? Explaining, on paper, what makes music great is not easy; writing about rock is often compared to "dancing about architecture."

Unlike the other rock milestones to which it is often compared, *Born to Run* cannot be considered an artistic or even a musical advance beyond what had appeared before it. It is no *Sergeant Pepper*, no *Highway 61*, no *Tommy*, no *Pet Sounds*. Rather it was — and remains — perhaps the most powerful explication of the pure spirit of rock 'n' roll that any artist has been able to capture since the night in July 1954 at the Sun Records studio in Memphis, when an unknown nineteen-year-old kid with the unlikely name of Elvis Presley let loose on Arthur "Big Boy" Crudup's "That's All Right." Leaving aside some of the unwelcome excesses of both progressive rock and puerile pop radio, *Born to Run* somehow manages to evoke the whole rock story line, both musically and lyrically, in the ultimate rock 'n' roll synthesis. Its crystal-clear "wall of sound" production improves on Phil Spector. Its harmonies require no apologies to Roy Orbison and Brian Wilson. Steve Van Zandt's horn arrangements echo the great achievements of the great Stax soul masterpieces. The opening riff of "Born to

Run" stands with the first few chords of "Layla," "Like a Rolling Stone," and "(I Can't Get No) Satisfaction" as the signature chords of rock 'n' roll. And the passionate delivery of Springsteen's hoarse, blistering vocals hold their own alongside young Elvis, Mick Jagger, and sometimes even Otis Redding. It's as if Bruce is playing on the home court of every icon of rock history, on the one hand paying his respects but on the other deepening their achievements and daring all of us to believe again in the entire collective enterprise.

Lyrically, Bruce has explained, he "was entrenched in classic rock 'n' roll images, and wanted to find a way to use those images without feeling anachronistic." The songs recite the familiar liturgies of rock 'n' roll: cars, dances, dreams, romance, danger, and escape. These themes, however, are treated with a degree of maturity and personal insight that enable them to ring true to those doing the dreaming as well as to those who feel that their dreams died with their diploma, first paycheck, or child. "It was the album where I left behind my adolescent definitions of love and freedom," Springsteen has since observed.

The poetry and power of *Born to Run* lie in its unwillingness to compromise, in the refusal of its protagonists to accept passively the hand dealt to them by circumstance. They lie in the passion brought to common struggles, a passion that is mirrored by the ferocious roar of the music. Mary, Terry, Wendy, and the Magic Rat are consistently searching within themselves, hoping to find the emotional resources — the love, the hope, the faith — to become their own heroes, to go on dreaming in the face of broken dreams. The album's stories are internal monologues and dramatic renderings of Springsteen's own personal struggles with his parents, with authority, with women, and with the expectations of the world, universalized and ennobled through the language of the radio on top of his mother's refrigerator. It is an album about the unsung heroism of everyday life, the quiet glory of unflinching personal integrity in a world where virtue is deemed to be its own reward.

Nearly a quarter-century later, *Born to Run* remains by far Springsteen's most popular album with his most devoted fans. In one 1993 poll the album not only topped all others by a considerable margin, but four of its eight songs occupied the top four positions and nearly 60 percent of the votes cast for "best song of all time in any category."* The album's title song was chosen to be the greatest rock song of all time by a 1995 panel of British music journalists, musicians, and songwriters

Born to Run received 36 percent of the votes for best album, followed by *Darkness on the Edge of Town*, with 25 percent. The voting order for best song came out: 1. "Thunder Road" (25 percent); 2. "Backstreets" (12 percent); 3. "Born to Run" (12 percent); 4. "Jungleland" (8 percent); 5. "Incident" (5 percent). (*Backstreets* 44, Fall 1993.) These results were closely replicated in a 1996 Internet poll of "LuckyTown Digest" subscribers. *Born to Run* received 31 percent of the first-place votes, followed by 22 percent for *Darkness*. The top five songs were "Thunder Road," "Born to Run," "Backstreets," and "Jungleland," followed by "Badlands" from *Darkness*.

organized by *The Times* of London and the BBC's Radio
1, where it edged out "Like a Rolling Stone." Eleven
years earlier it had finished second to "Stairway to
Heaven" in a WNEW-FM listeners' poll, with "Thunder
Road" and "Jungleland" coming in at numbers thirteen
and sixteen, respectively. Of the three original songs
Bruce chose to play when he was inducted into the Rock
'n' Roll Hall of Fame in March 1999, two were from *Born
to Run*, "Tenth Avenue Freeze-Out" and Backstreets."

Springsteen was emotionally unprepared for anything
like the publicity blitz that his masterpiece — and its
accompanying media campaign — inspired. When asked
earlier that year what he would do if he became rich
from his labors, Springsteen had to stop and think. "If I
was rich? If I made a lot of money, you mean? Let me
think. Phew! I'd get my mother to quit working. My father to quit working. My mother's been working since
she was eighteen — she's fifty now. It's too long to work.
Right off, that's all I can think of."

Now, suddenly, he was a bona-fide "phenomenon,"
though according to Steve Van Zandt, neither he nor
Bruce knew whether the word began with a *p* or an *f*.
"Why should I be on the cover of *Newsweek?*" he asked
when he first heard the news. "I don't deserve it. That's
for presidents."

The hype nearly crushed Springsteen. Before his first
London appearance, Springsteen tore down "Future of
Rock & Roll" posters in the lobby of the Hammersmith

Odeon. He then gave a near comatose performance, probably his worst ever, before returning a few weeks later and ripping the roof off the same venue. Walking through a county fair in Phoenix, he told one writer, "Everybody wants to spend all their time talkin' about what we're doin'. All I want to do is do it, but it's getting harder and harder. . . . I mean, all I ever wanted to do was make records, have a band like this. I don't want this other stuff, ya know."

The "other stuff" was a pain, but part of the price he had to pay for the prize he had won. On one extraordinary occasion in Memphis, he even tried to cash in on it. Here is the story in Bruce's own words:

It was real late at night, and we were looking for something to eat. We get in the cab with this guy and said, "Listen, we wanna eat." It was me and Miami Steve. And this guy says, "I know, I'll take you to Fridays." Well, we don't want, like, a hangout, we wanna place to go and eat, ya know? So he says, "There's a place out by Elvis's house. . . ." We say, "Out by Elvis — TAKE US THERE RIGHT NOW!" He says, "You guys celebrities?" We say, "Yeah, yeah." "Can I tell my dispatcher I got celebrities?" "Sure, sure." [Laughs.] He gets on the thing and says, "Joe, Joe, I got . . . ," and shoves the mike in my face cuz he don't know who we are. [Laughs.]

I say, "Bruce Springsteen, E Street Band, from New Jersey, blah, blah," and the cab driver says, "We're going out to Elvis." The dispatcher says, "Damn! Damn!" 'cause he thinks we're going to have coffee with Elvis or something. [Laughs.] So we get out there, and I stood in front of those gates. He's got a big long driveway, and I looked up and saw a light on and I said, "I gotta find out if he's home, Steve, I can't stand it." I jumped over the wall — a stone wall — and I hear the cabdriver say, "Man, they got DOGS in there!" I ran up the driveway, and there was nobody. I ran up to the front door and I knocked. From out of the woods, I see somebody watching me, so I figure I'll just go over to the guy to say, "Hello, I just came to see Elvis. . . ." So out comes this security guy, says, "What are ya doing?" I said, "Well, I'm in a band. I play guitar. I came to see Elvis." And he tells me, "Elvis ain't home. He's in Lake Tahoe." I say, "Are you sure?" He says, "Yeah." "Well," I said, "if he comes back, tell him Bruce Springsteen . . ." But the guard didn't know me from nobody. I tell him, "Listen, I was in *Time, Newsweek*." And he says, "Yeah, sure." [Laughs.] "You gotta go outside now." And he took me to the bottom of the gate and dumped me back out on the street.

The leader of the world's greatest rock 'n' roll band, it turned out, was nothing more than a starstruck twenty-six-year-old kid trying to jump the fence at Graceland to get a glimpse of his hero.

I built that Challenger by myself

But I needed money so I sold it.

I lived a secret I should have kept to myself

But I got drunk one night and I told it

— "The Promise," 1976

No Surrender

The massive Springsteen hype, following the release of *Born to Run*, continually competed with the backlash against it. *Newsweek* felt compelled to explain to its readers why it published a cover story on an unknown rock singer the same week its most prominent competitor did. *Time*'s managing editor, Henry Grunwald, was heard grumbling that putting Springsteen on the cover the same week *Newsweek* did was the most embarrassing decision of his tenure there as editor. (He was eight years into the job.) Other performers were annoyed by all the attention Springsteen received, as well. Stephen Stills complained, "This Bruce Springsteen stuff drives me crazy. He's nowhere as good as his hype." Bob Geldof added, in a no less self-revealing tone, "Bruce Springsteen couldn't write a song as good as 'Rat Trap' if he tried. I don't believe Springsteen. He writes fiction. The Magic Rat did not drive his sleek machine over the Jersey state line."

And Springsteen himself grew increasingly upset by the argument that he was a critically invented one-hit wonder. "That bothered me a lot," he later admitted. "Being perceived as an invention, a ship passing by. I'd been playing for ten years. I knew where I came from, every inch of the way."

Springsteen's career, meanwhile, entered a kind of professional purgatory. Between 1976 and 1978, on both coasts and in parts of the Midwest, he was not merely a superstar but a superstar at the frenzied height of his career, like Elvis in 1956 or Dylan a decade later. Bruce would go to the movies near his home in New Jersey and leave to find fans lined up outside the theater. Some writers would get so excited in his presence that they could hardly contain themselves. "Jeezez Christ! We're rolling down the highway with fuckin' Bruce Springsteen at the wheel! And he's driving the way you would think Bruce Springsteen would drive" was the way an overjoyed Mike Greenblatt put in the New Jersey *Aquarian*. One promoter offered Springsteen a guaranteed payday of half a million dollars to headline a July 4, 1976, bicentennial bash at the 80,000-seat JFK Stadium in Philadelphia.

Disgusted by much of the attention, Bruce did his best to subvert it. Fearing a loss of intimacy with his audience, he refused to play halls that seated more than 3,000 people. At the time Springsteen announced six nights at New York's 2,800-seat Palladium in late autumn 1976 — the first chance New Yorkers had to see him since the Bottom Line hysteria — he undoubtedly could have sold out the 20,000-seat Madison Square Garden instead. Nor would he agree to appear on television despite what Mike Appel reported was an offer in excess of a million dollars from NBC for a one-hour performance. The media did all the Asbury Park music scene stories they could. Southside Johnny and the Asbury Jukes got a major-label record deal, with Steve Van Zandt producing. And then, suddenly, for the next three years the Great White Hope disappeared.

The reason was Mike Appel, who had been trying to blackball Landau, whom he viewed as stealing his creation away. He was also withholding money from Springsteen and pressuring him to extend their contract for another five years. Appel controlled all the money CBS was turning over to Springsteen, including a half-million-dollar advance, now that his considerable debts to the company had been honored. But Bruce had finally figured out that he was getting paid approximately one-tenth of what he earned, and he hired an auditor to look at Appel's books, such as they were. The auditor's verdict was that Appel's professional conduct had been "slipshod, wasteful and neglectful . . . a classic case of the unconscionable exploitation of an unsophisticated and unrepresented performer by his manager."

Less than a year after the breakthrough Bottom Line gigs, on July 27, 1976, Springsteen fired Appel and sued him in federal court in Manhattan for fraud and undue influence. Two days later Appel countersued in New

York State Supreme Court. The now ex-manager also convinced Judge Arnold L. Fein to issue a preliminary injunction enjoining Springsteen from entering the studio with Jon Landau while the case was being decided. The injunction was upheld on appeal, and Springsteen was therefore barred from making his next record with his chosen producer. Rather than let Appel dictate terms, he decided not to record at all until the lawsuit was settled.

The court battle that followed was a drama that had been played out over and over throughout the history of pop music, from the days of perpetually impoverished R&B singers in the forties and fifties through the troubles that kept the great John Fogerty out of the studio during most of the 1980s. The wonderful low-budget Jamaican reggae film *The Harder They Come*, released in 1972 and starring Jimmy Cliff, turns on exactly this issue, leading its protagonist to become an outlaw when his music is taken away from him.

According to the published depositions, Appel's lawyer, Leonard Marks, questioned Springsteen in his office conference room with the goal of demonstrating that the star had been overly cavalier about money. These exchanges tend to be simultaneously comical and painful, since Bruce cared nothing about money and knew even less. Asked whether it was wasteful to insist on a hotel when the band was traveling in a camper, Bruce explained, "It's like this, Mr. Marks. Did you ever sleep with seven guys in a station wagon like this? Do you know what that's like for eight hours? We needed a bus." Marks requested that the answer be struck as unresponsive. Bruce was also challenged about why he had not proved more cooperative with Appel's various money-making schemes, a line of questioning that did not appeal to the artist: "I can make twenty bucks for dropping my pants on Broadway, too, but I don't do it." Questioned about his rejection of Appel's idea of doing a national tour with a traveling tent, Springsteen responded, "You want to do law in a tent? I will not play my guitar in a tent." Examined about his refusal to play the Cole Field House even after Appel tried to put curtains up to improve the sound, Bruce told the lawyer, "You can put curtains in a whorehouse, too, and it is still a whorehouse." The deposition continued in this vein. Marks wanted to know if Springsteen knew how much his "valet" was paid. "I don't have no valet," Bruce insisted. "I don't have people kissing my ass." Marks wondered whether Bruce knew how much his staffers were paid. Bruce explained that when one of them complained that he wasn't making enough money, the artist told him to "take more," without having any idea — or even asking — how much the man earned in the first place. Springsteen also admitted that he had not paid much attention when he signed his first contract with Appel; he had no idea, for example, what publishing rights were when he gave them to Appel. When Marks tried to put Springsteen on the spot as to whether he could point to any specific evidence of Appel's actually having "cheated" him, Bruce tried to impress upon the lawyer that the question was misplaced. "All I know," he explained, "I don't own a ——— thing that I ever wrote. He told me I had half my publishing, and he lied to me. . . . I wrote 'Born to Run,' every line of that ——— song is me, and no line of that ——— song is his. I don't own it. I can't print it on a piece of paper if I wanted to."

Springsteen became so excited when trying to explain how critical this issue was to him that he jumped on the conference table and began screaming. "I don't own [anything]," he yelled. "I don't own any of that stuff. Man, that is my blood in the thing. That is mine. I lived every ——— line of that song. Do you understand that? I lived every ——— line of that."

According to Leonard Marks, Springsteen then leaped off the table and ran into the ladies' bathroom, mistaking it for the men's room. When he returned, slightly calmer, Marks asked Springsteen if, in fact, given his contractual obligations, it was not he — not Appel — who had broken his word. Bruce screamed back: "I'll tell you one thing, you got a lot of ——— balls to sit there about my breaking my ——— word, when he did to me, he ——— lied to me up and down. When I signed them original contracts, he told me, 'These things mean nothing. Sign it. Trust me and sign these ——— things.' That's his exact words. 'These things mean nothing.' I broke my ——— word? He broke his ——— word. Somebody stabs me in the ——— heart. I learn to stab them back in the ——— heart."

Deciding he had taken all the "abuse" he intended to

take, Marks then shut down the deposition, complaining, "It is a shame the record can't reflect some of the drama that took place here today." In a truly bizarre development, Marks and the ten or so lawyers involved in the case representing Appel, Springsteen, Columbia, and Jon Landau then proceeded together to the judge's office to try to find some way to continue the proceedings in a more orderly fashion. Judge Fein asked to speak to Springsteen privately. Bruce returned from Fein's study considerably subdued; according to one report, the judge simply informed him that everything he said — profanities and all — was being taken down and recorded for posterity, which Bruce apparently had no idea was the case.

According to Springsteen partisans, the case turned on December 8, when he submitted an affidavit explaining why, as an artist, it was so important to him to choose his own collaborators. Bruce explained to the judge that "my interest is in my career, which up until now holds the promise of my being able to significantly contribute to, and possibly influence, a generation of music. No amount of money could compensate me if I were to lose this opportunity."

After just under a year of legal jockeying, the two parties settled the suit in a marathon meeting that ended at 3:00 A.M. on May 28, 1977. Though he may have had the upper hand legally, Appel really had no choice but to settle, for Springsteen made it clear that he would never work with him again. The details were never officially released, but Appel later claimed to have received

$800,000 in cash, plus a share of future profits from the first three albums, along with a five-year production deal with Columbia.* Bruce Springsteen won control of his catalog and the right to work with any producer he wanted. Days later Springsteen signed a new agreement with Columbia and went back into the studio with Landau to get back to the task at hand.

And here is where our fairy tale ends. The lawsuit, and the entire *Born to Run* experience, transformed Springsteen and darkened his vision of life. While starving for his music had not tested his faith, being forced to testify in court against a former friend and mentor who he felt had cheated him certainly did. Springsteen was no longer quite the same person who had walked into the studio three years earlier. He entered a romantic young innocent and left a guarded, distrustful adult. "Trusting is a weird, tricky business," he told a reporter in 1977. "I guess what I am asking is maybe an impossible thing to ask of anybody. I mean, there's trust and there's *trust*, you know? . . . Everyone has a breaking point."

Springsteen admitted that he had undergone "a big awakening" during this period, during which he "realized a lot of things about [his] past." Twenty-eight years old, he discovered that the running and just running some more so idealized on *Born to Run* was no answer.

---

*Appel said he eventually sold his share of the publishing rights back to Springsteen for $425,000. His production deal never resulted in any notable success.

"Where were these two people going?" he finally asked himself. "I didn't know myself." From that moment on, Bruce Springsteen began to construct his own story line. He wanted "control right now," he took it, and he paid the price. The story Bruce had in mind did not include being anyone's messiah — at least not anytime soon. The artist had constantly warned about the dangers of looking for "saviors" to clean up the messy lives of individuals. In "Song to the Orphans," recorded for *Greetings* but not released, he sings that "the lost souls search for saviors but saviors don't last long." In "Thunder Road" he famously warns Mary not to "waste [her] summers praying in vain for a savior to rise from these streets." Springsteen did not want to make a heroic album; as Jon Landau explained, "If success was what it was like with *Born to Run,* Bruce didn't want that. He didn't want to have one song that could be taken out of context and interfere with what he wanted the album to represent." What Springsteen did want was to make an album true to the confusion he was feeling in his soul at that moment in his life. He sought "to strip away the illusion . . . to strip away the fairy tale."

The musical universe in which Springsteen created *Darkness on the Edge of Town* was a much-changed place in the three years since he had made his last appearance. The rise of punk on the one hand and disco on the other had simultaneously polarized popular music and energized it. *Rolling Stone* dated the moment that disco crossed over to white audiences to August 1975, the very month of Springsteen's Bottom Line performances, though Studio 54 did not open until April 1977. The birth of the American punk movement can be conveniently pinned to the release of the Ramones' first album in June 1976, though of course it was germinating earlier. Each movement seemed to define itself as the negative image of the other. Punk was white, teenage, angry, uncompromising, and unwilling to prettify itself to the point of even refusing putting on clean clothes. (Springsteen had frequently been called a punk in the pre-punk days, but this definition had a more wholesome 1950s/Marlon Brando/*West Side Story* connotation.) Seventies punks did not dance; they thrashed. The performers spat at the audience, and the audience spat back or, if they were in a nasty mood, threw bottles. Punk performers tried to outdo one another in self-abnegation and aggressive nihilist politics. Many of the performers who began as punks, however, demonstrated tremendous talent and originality. The Sex Pistols and the Ramones produced terrific debut albums that enriched rock's canon and reinvigorated its rebellious spirit, before the former imploded and the latter collapsed into comedic shtick. The Clash, Patti Smith, Elvis Costello, Tom Verlaine, David Johansen, and the Talking Heads, meanwhile, grew into a genuine artistic vanguard as they learned to transcend punk's stifling strictures and combine it with other musical and philosophical influences.

Disco shared with punk a romantic relationship with narcotics — in this case, cocaine. Musically, it was everything punk was not. Punk was white while disco was black. Disco musicians dressed to the nines and sang of love and sex, of "good times." The entire philosophical foundation of the music could be summed up in the incessantly repeated phrase "get down tonight."Authenticity, so crucial to the punk ethos that even technical proficiency was considered suspect, was simply not an issue for disco. Some of the bands with top-ten records did not exist as such, but were simply studio musicians working with a hot producer who knew what he wanted.

The net result of the popularity of these two musical movements was a collapse in the center. *Born to Run* had revived hopes for a rebirth of rock among critics and fans, but these proved short-lived. Bob Seger slipped through the door with the wonderful Springsteenesque "Night Moves." Stevie Wonder kept chugging along, turning out masterpiece after masterpiece, and the Stones found a second creative wind in 1978 with the release of the disco-tinged *Some Girls*. Dylan, too, experienced a brief period of rejuvenation with 1975's magisterial *Blood on the Tracks*, but soon afterward he seemed to lose his artistic direction entirely. His indecipherably self-involved four-and-a-half-hour film, *Renaldo and Clara*, was followed by a period in which the middle-class, Jewish-born poet became a born-again Christian evangelist. Meanwhile, Elvis Presley died of bloat and self-indulgence, after having ended his career as the world's worst Elvis imitator.

The artistic ups and downs of the performers aside, most of the unhappy developments in the music industry during the second half of the seventies involved its simultaneous homogenization and corporatization. The business grew enormously during this period, and showers of money fell on both artists and executives. As early as 1973, a *Rolling Stone* cover story welcomed its readers "to the Wide Open World of the Corporate Dead," picking perhaps the most potent symbol of counterculture antimaterialism — the Grateful Dead — to demonstrate the ubiquity of the capitalist contagion which had in fact long ago swallowed the magazine itself. Rock stars began to believe that they constituted some new form of royalty. As Eagle Glenn Frey, one of the anointed, remembered, "That was the music business at its decadent zenith. I remember Don [Henley] had a birthday in Cincinnati, and they flew in cases of Château Lafite Rothschild. I seem to remember that the wine was the best and the drugs were good and the women were beautiful, and we seemed to have an endless amount of energy. Hangovers were conquered with Bloody Marys."

Artistically, empty spectacle was the norm, and the emptier the better, as demonstrated by the forty-foot inflatable pig that British art rockers Pink Floyd used as a stage prop. Another telling symbol of the period was the decision of the Doobie Brothers — a band, after all, whose name was inspired by marijuana — to sponsor the first ever rock 'n' roll golf tournament. The Marshall Tucker Band started a trend by agreeing to tour on behalf of a corporate sponsor, Pabst Blue Ribbon beer. It was during these years that rock also married mainstream politics. President Ford tried to improve his "youth" credibility by inviting Peter Frampton to the White House just before the 1976 election. Down South, the Allman Brothers Band performed concerts for Jimmy Carter. ("Would Brother Greg be appointed to head the Food and Drug Administration?" went the joke at the time.)

No longer even pretending to be a form of rebellion, rock music was now second only to film as the most powerful financial force in the entertainment industry. It is therefore fitting that it offered up perhaps the most extreme example of what the scholar Christopher Lasch called in 1978 the "culture of narcissism." It was a culture, Lasch observed, "of competitive individualism, which in its decadence has carried the logic of individualism to an extreme of war against all, the pursuit of happiness to the dead end of a narcissistic preoccupation with the self." By the end of the 1970s, Lasch noted, "the invasion of private life by the forces of organized domination has become so pervasive that personal life has almost ceased to exist."

Though its approach could hardly be more different than that of a philosopher/social critic, Springsteen's

Darkness on the Edge of Town may be profitably viewed as a response to many of the same social phenomena diagnosed in Lasch's *Culture of Narcissism*. But in confronting the central dogmas of the age, Springsteen was putting himself in a complicated artistic position. He was calling for resistance to a problem he could not define: to a "crossfire [he didn't] understand." *Darkness on the Edge of Town* is an album about responding to unseen and undefinable forms of domination and repression. But Springsteen makes no attempt to blame the people who actually exercise authority in the system. They, too, are caught in the same web, and unable to recognize, much less struggle against it. These are everyday people, Springsteen has explained, who are "stretching for the light in the darkness, just people trying to hold on to the things they believe in the face of the battering from outside." The album is filled with faces "that have had the humanity beaten out of them. . . . The guy with the crazy eyes." These are people who are "already six feet under, people with nothin' to lose and full of poison. I try to write about the other choice they had."

Saul Bellow's 1976 Nobel lecture made the point that writers had given up "the connection of literature with the main human enterprise." This was clearly not true of Bruce Springsteen. In returning to the studio with Jon Landau, Springsteen aimed to record an album whose heart, he said, lay "somewhere between *Born to Run*'s spiritual hopefulness and seventies cynicism." If so, it was the latter that dominated, though the former never admitted defeat. The new record, Springsteen had re-solved, "couldn't be a warm, innocent album" like *Born to Run* because "it wasn't that way for me anymore. That's why a lot of pain had to be there, because it's real, because it happens." Embodying that pain were charac-ters who felt "weathered, older, but not beaten. The sense of daily struggle in each song greatly increased. The possibility of transcendence or any sort of personal redemption felt a lot harder to come by. This was the tone I wanted to sustain. I intentionally steered away from any hint of escapism and set my characters down in the middle of a community under siege."

Once again Springsteen spent more than a year pre-paring the album. He wrote and recorded an enormous number of songs, but eventually rejected all those — in-cluding the great ones — that he felt compromised its bleak mood. There are no happy or even remotely frivo-lous songs on *Darkness*. Springsteen said he "didn't make room for certain things because I just couldn't un-derstand how you could feel so good and so bad at the same time. And it was very confusing to me."

The songs on *Darkness* are about the characters *Born to Run* left behind. The record turns on an axis of anger; each song focuses on the desire to break bonds that have become chains, while lamenting the losses such a break necessitates. It is about recognizing that anger and ha-tred and the turning away of one's heart are the logical responses to the forces that claw away at your soul, but not the only possible ones. It is an album about the power of individual faith, of perseverance, of heart (but not, quite clearly, of love), to find a place to make a stand, however small and unlikely to succeed. Two kinds of people live in Springsteen's *Darkness* universe: "guys [who] just give up living / and start dying little by little, piece by piece," and "guys [who] come home from work and wash up / And go racin' in the street."

Much of the anguish Springsteen experienced during his lawsuit is discernible between the lines of the lyrics on *Darkness*, though no explicit references are made to any part of it. He even removed from the album "The Promise," one of the songs most beloved by fans, because it was being interpreted by many who heard it in concert as a comment on the suit. "I don't write songs about lawsuits," he angrily commented at the time, when the issue was raised.

The album's central thematic pivot is Springsteen's rage at the matrix of arbitrary authority that destroys our youthful hopes and dreams as we enter adulthood. But unlike the class-conscious anthems of adolescent anger he performed in concert — "It's My Life" and "We Gotta Get Out of This Place" — these songs empathize with those caught inside the web of authority as well as those seeking to find some firm ground for resistance to it. Foremost among these figures is Springsteen's father, the character around whom much of the action on *Darkness* revolves. The two men were "prisoners of love, a love in chains . . . / With the same hot blood burning in [their] veins." Springsteen's "daddy worked his whole life for nothing but the pain / Now he walks these empty rooms looking for something to blame." His son "inherit[s] the sins [and] inherit[s] the flames," but not his passivity. "Mister, I ain't a boy, no I'm a man," he sings, not as the kind of unintentionally self-revealing braggadocio we heard on "It's Hard to Be a Saint in the City," but as a statement of fact: a crucial assertion of individuality and identity. He may not understand the socioeconomic structure that imprisoned his father, but he is determined not to let whatever it was that destroyed his spirit take control of his, as well. "I don't give a damn / For the same old played out scenes / I don't give a damn / For just the in-betweens / Honey, I want the heart, / I want the soul / I want control right now." The power of the album's stinging guitar and soaring saxophone solos insists that its protagonist will charge into a brick wall over and over again, until it gives way and his virtual prison cell crumbles and falls. "Blow away the dreams that tear you apart," he sings. "Blow away the dreams that break your heart / Blow away the lies that leave you nothing but lost and brokenhearted."

But who created the "badlands" and how can you escape them? Who is this "mister" who keeps insisting that Bruce is just a boy, and not a man? Who owns the factory that destroyed his father's spirit, and why do the men walk out with "death in their eyes"? Is the problem capitalism? Work itself? Would the workers still have deathly eyes if they were represented by powerful, militant unions, such as the UAW or the CIO during their respective heydays? What if the company established worker-ownership committees or employee stock options? None of these questions are asked, much less answered. This is, the songwriter seems to tell us, just the way things are.

Although *Darkness*'s production is considerably less grandiose, like *Born to Run* the album is filled with triumphant boasts and soaring musical crescendos. But they are always tempered, if not undercut, by the possibility that the narrator is kidding himself — or that the victories are temporary but the war permanent. As Springsteen himself has observed of the album, "There's more of a sense of: 'If you wanna ride, you're gonna pay.'"

The "you" addressed on *Darkness* is always singular, never plural, much less communal. Hence the response to every defeat, every broken heart, and every dashed dream is always the same: the individual must simply will him- or herself the strength to go on. There are no political answers on this album; no community upon which to rely or family to turn to for help. Romantic love, it must be added, is hardly present at all on the album. There is the lone individual and there is the void: the "darkness on the edge of town."

The key to life is to avoid getting caught in the crossfire, not letting the badlands, the factory, that something in the night, the brokenhearted dreams, keep you from getting back to the business of dreaming again. It's a nasty world, one narrator after another tells us, and you have to fight back to preserve the right to keep dreaming, to keep living your life even if the hopes embodied in your dreams are mocked and trampled. "If dreams came true, oh, wouldn't that be nice," he sings sarcastically. "But this ain't no dream we're living through tonight / Girl, you want it, you take it, you pay the price."

The lyrics on *Darkness* are hardly the only source of its otherworldly power. As Joyce Millman would note in an appreciation penned nearly twenty years later, "the music is like Phil Spector melted down and mixed with background gravel to model a new kind of folk music." But it's an "urban folk music," she explains, "that quotes rock and roll the way Jimmie Rodgers and Hank Williams quoted black and Appalachian spirituals." The songs are anchored by music that is almost formalistic in its devotion to the basic structures of the three- and four-chord power riff. The melodies plod occasionally, but they never break the mood established by the record's uncompromising lyrics. Once again, by mining the roots of rock's past and blending it through his own psyche and experiences on *Darkness*, Springsteen succeeded in taking something old and making it feel new again.

Still intensely sensitive to the hype charge, Springsteen tried desperately to protect his creation from the curse of commercialism. In addition to the unrelentingly dour tone of the music, he chose for its cover shot a portrait taken by his friend, Frank Stefanko, who worked full-time in a south Jersey meat market. It is shot against the wall in Stefanko's bedroom, and Bruce looks as if he might be in a coma. The release date was delayed when Springsteen decided at the last minute to add a Steve Van Zandt guitar solo to "Promised Land" and, hence, remix the entire album. When it was finally completed, he asked Columbia to agree to release it with absolutely no publicity.

Critically, reaction to the album was highly favorable, if not quite ecstatic. Most of the critics who loved *Born to Run* loved *Darkness* as well, but not as passionately or perhaps as innocently. One interviewer told Springsteen, "I was surprised that there weren't any razor blades attached to the LP." *Crawdaddy*'s Peter Knobler found "enough raw emotion to make you shake; several songs to take with you to your grave." Jay Cocks, writing in *Time,* believed Bruce was "not just reaffirming his promise as the preeminent rock figure of the late '70s, but redeeming, even enhancing it."

The release of *Darkness* deepened Springsteen's relationship with his fan base considerably. The three years between albums had seemed interminable to many, but the music's uncompromising integrity and undeniable power made the wait worthwhile. While not as obviously anthemic or redemptive as *Born to Run, Darkness* was no less transportative, and occasionally transcendent. It spoke to the mood of the culture without condescending to it. "Badlands," "Adam Raised a Cain,"

"Promised Land," and "Racing in the Street" belong at the top of the Springsteen canon.

Drawn ever more powerfully to the unique and inimitable experience that his music offered us, Springsteen fans of various ages and emotional states were increasingly taking on the characteristics of what the New England Puritans called an "invisible church." We traveled great distances for the ecstatic experience of his performance. We turned to his songs for inspiration, for consolation, and for insight into our own lives — for advice about how to deal with our parents, our friends, our lovers, our anger and disappointments. We pored over the lyrics for hidden meanings and argued about the "correct" interpretations. Writing about those days in the *Iowa Review*, Hope Edelman describes the world of Springsteen's invisible church in its suburban adolescent incarnation.

Even the most intelligent, even the most affluent, among us had visions of a utopia free of parents, P.E. teachers, and pop quizzes. Springsteen offered us his version of that place, his promises surrounding us like audio wallpaper — hogging the airwaves on our car radios, piped into our homerooms, pumped into every store in our local indoor shopping mall, encircling us with songs of hot desire and escape. . . . The songs that gave you hope there was a simpler, gentler world out there somewhere, and that the happiness missing from your own backyard could be found in the next town . . . back when you thought Bruce Springsteen knew a lot about you, as you lay alone on your twin bed with the door slammed shut and the hif-fi turned up to 9.

Twenty years after its release, *Darkness* still holds a firm place as Springsteen's second most popular record with his fans. Certainly few were surprised or disappointed when he opened up with "Promised Land" immediately after his induction speech at the Rock and Roll Hall of Fame ceremony in March 1999. But the quantum increase in the power of Springsteen's reputation and the size and dedication of his fan base during this period can hardly be attributed only or even largely to *Darkness*. Rather it was the constant touring the band had undertaken when the court forbade it to record. Sometimes called the "Chicken Scratch tour," sometimes called the "Lawsuit tour," it played in medium-size halls rather than in clubs, and continued to build Springsteen's performing legend. He played everywhere, from the *Crawdaddy* tenth anniversary party to every rinky-dink college on the circuit. One night he even played a free concert at the enormously unlikely location of the Connecticut prep school Choate where, according to one observer, he put on "one of the greatest rock shows of all time" purely as a tribute to the school's distinguished alumnus, John Hammond. Springsteen described his ambition as a refusal to give people merely their money's worth. "You don't go out there to deliver $7.50 worth of music," he explained. "My whole thing is to deliver what money could not possibly buy."

Audiences and critics alike sensed this fact, and Springsteen — through word of mouth rather than hype this time — had soon built up the largest and most devoted cult audience in rock music. Peter Oppel, writing in the *Dallas Morning News*, caught the mood precisely: "The last time I reviewed a Bruce Springsteen concert, I had to meet an early deadline and I was caught up in the excitement of the moment. I was forced to compose a review in the middle of the concert with sights and sounds swirling around me even as I wrote. Superlatives gushed from my head like oil from the backyard of a Saudi Arabian family. No such pressures are upon me these days. Cooler heads can prevail. The code words are calm, collected. So now, in full control of my faculties, I can calmly and coolly say a Bruce Springsteen concert is the greatest show in the history of rock 'n' roll."

Though Springsteen acceded to playing hockey arenas during this period — it was the only way he could accommodate the ticket demand and foil scalpers — he did none of the typical rock-star turns. During every show, he and Clemons would, together, wade deep into the audience during "Spirit in the Night" as if to break down any remaining barriers between who he was and who he had become. When security workers would appear to be overly rough with particularly enthusiastic members of the audience, he would look down and yell, "Get outta here. These guys are my friends," later explaining to a journalist, "I can't watch kids getting knocked down in the front row, because that's me. That's a part of me."

Springsteen never liked "The Fever," but he played it on the *Darkness* tour in many cities because, he said, "people would jump onstage and grab me by the head and

scream, 'Bruce! Fever!'" Springsteen also added an intermission to the show, noting that "until someone said
the Allman Brothers did one, it never crossed my mind.
I never did an intermission in my life. I figured, what do
you need an intermission for?" Then he realized, "We
could actually do more if we did an intermission. Play
more songs. Do more!"

The show grew longer and the crowds more ecstatic.
In an interview with a Philadelphia radio station, he was
asked if he had any final words for his fans. Bruce responded, a little sheepishly, "I just want to say that the
crowds were fantastic. But I wish that all the girls [laugh-
ing] would not jump up and kiss me when I'm singing. It
sounds funny, but it's true, because you can't sing when
somebody jumps up and kisses ya and all that sorta stuff.
So if you can all just stay down, off the stage, it would be
appreciated. I don't like to have security in front, so I
sort of depend on the fans to be OK. Less kissing would
be appreciated."

Springsteen finally reconciled himself to playing
three nights at Madison Square Garden at the end of the
summer of 1978. I remember getting my eighteen-year-
old self arrested on the first of those nights, just before I
left for college, because, as I explained to a rather bemused member of New York City's finest, I was trying to
give Bruce my old high-top sneakers, as a symbol of how
much "Born to Run" had meant to me. ("Bruce Springsteen doesn't want your ugly old sneakers, you dumb
kid," the cop rather wisely observed, before letting me

off with a warning.) The next year, as a college freshman, I carried out an elaborate and brilliantly choreographed plan to leave a short story I had written about him in his dressing room. At another show on that tour, I was forced to risk my life by lying down in the aisle, as I had traveled the two hundred miles to see the band while stricken with mononucleosis.

What was it about Bruce that made me behave this way? Why did a fortyish woman in New Orleans hand him her grandmother's engagement ring from the pit below the stage?* It is no easier to explain today than it was two decades ago. After seeing Springsteen perform in Boston in 1978, Paul Nelson attempted an explanation. The performance, he wrote, "made me fall in love with rock 'n' roll again. Here's this guy who just spent a year breaking his back on a new album, who'd gone straight into a four-month tour, and you couldn't pay him enough not to play for almost three hours. Every night. No matter where. Or to whom." Nelson noted that after playing a triumphant "Born to Run," "when the crowd offers him a tremendous ovation, he subverts the applause by holding up his guitar as if it were some communal inducement of magic, something which he alone does not own. All of a sudden I realized that we are making this glorious noise not for the pride of one man but for the power of rock 'n' roll."

---

* Bruce left it with the management of the hall the next day, with instructions to return the ring to the woman if she should have a change of heart and come looking for it.

Greil Marcus would later discern from a broader perspective why a Bruce Springsteen concert proved such a powerful antidote to the rest of life. In his brilliant "Presliad" essay, published in *Mystery Train*, Marcus had argued that Elvis "almost has the scope to take America in." Now, however,

Rock and roll is, today, too big for any center. It is so big, in fact, that no single event — be it Springsteen's tour or Sid Vicious' overdose — can be much more than peripheral. Writing in August 1977, Lester Bangs may have got it right: "We will never again agree on anything as we agreed on Elvis." Rock and roll now has less an audience than a series of increasingly discrete audiences, and those various audiences ignore each other. . . . In one sense, this is salutary and inevitable. The lack of a center means the lack of a conventional definition of what rock and roll is, and that fosters novelty . . . but this state of affairs is also debilitating and dispiriting. The fact that the most adventurous music of the day seems to have taken up residence in the darker corners of the marketplace contradicts the idea of rock and roll as an aggressively popular culture that tears up boundaries of race, class, geography and (oh yes) music. . . . A concert by Bruce Springsteen offers many thrills, and one is that he performs as if none of the above is true.

What, finally, was the source of Springsteen's ability to face down a culture of narcissism, polarity, alienation, pessimism, and escapism? The evidence appears to suggest that it was no more than the supreme act of will he demanded of his characters on *Darkness*, and this was an enormous part of his appeal. Springsteen looked and acted just like his audience. He did not indulge groupies, drugs, hangers-on, or even limos. He was just a guy like you, though he had a better job. And if he could do it — if he could stare into the darkness and come out swinging and smiling, and dancing and telling jokes — well, then life must be worth living. "I had a big awakening in the past two, three years," Springsteen told an interviewer during the *Darkness* tour. "But I came out of it. You could see it onstage, the whole band's just full of too much life to throw it all away."

Rock 'n' roll, remember, is "never, never about surrender."

Hey ho, rock and roll, deliver me from nowhere

— "Open All Night," 1982

Nowhere Man

In the autumn of 1979, Bruce Springsteen caused a major rift in my family. In what turned out to be his only announced appearance during the more than two years he spent recording *The River*, Springsteen played a benefit with a group of L.A. rockers at Madison Square Garden to oppose nuclear energy. Because the Clash and the Who would also be in town the same week, I decided this rare opportunity outweighed the importance of any classes I might miss, and so I left college and went home outside New York City for a few days. My parents, who viewed college in terms of the investment they made in tuition and room and board, were not pleased, and Bruce and his fellow Musicians United for Safe Energy did not help matters much by scheduling the first of Springsteen's two shows on Kol Nidre, the holiest night of the Jewish calendar. I remember getting picked up hitchhiking to the train that night by the mother of an old basketball teammate named

Goldberg, who thought she was giving me a ride to meet my parents for services. When I told her the real story — that I was going to a Springsteen concert — she made me get out of the car and walk the last half mile to the train.

Rarely in history has a cause gone less recognized by those ostensibly assembled to support it. Nuclear power? Sure, it sucks, whatever. We were there to see Bruce. The performers who preceded him on the bill either rode the Springsteen wave or were swept under by it. Jackson Browne smartly joined the crowd in chanting, "Broooce," in between his own songs. Chaka Khan ran off the stage in tears. ("Broooce" apparently sounds a lot like "boo" when you're onstage.) "Too bad his name isn't Melvin," quipped Bonnie Raitt by way of meager consolation.

The fifty or so minutes it took the crew to set up the E Street Band's equipment after Jackson Browne finally left the stage felt like the longest night of my life. The longer Bruce took to come onstage, the greater the likelihood I would miss the last train home and end up sleeping outside Grand Central Station when they swept out its permanent denizens between 1:30 and 5:00 A.M. Springsteen and the E Street Band finally came on late, played a magnificent ninety-minute set, and forced me to pass Yom Kippur morning in Grand Central. Yet if the point of prayer is to inspire spiritual epiphany in the company of religious community, as the founder of Reconstructionist Judaism, Rabbi Mordecai Kaplan, argued, then I had been in the right place on Kol Nidre. This was not just music anymore. It was something bigger, more powerful, more . . . like a religion.

That show ended with Bruce mimicking Elvis's dance steps from "Jailhouse Rock," thereby channeling yet another key moment in the history of ur-rock 'n' roll. The band played, Bruce later said, "like a runaway train." All twenty thousand of us screamed and danced together with no thought except how lucky we felt to be there. Nukes or no nukes, Kol Nidre or no Nidre, if there was a God, he would have to understand: It ain't no sin to be glad you're alive.

No Nukes occurred during another of Springsteen's "I'm going to make the perfect rock 'n' roll record if it takes me the entire decade" phases, which meant that his new releases were separated by approximately three years. While these waits felt interminable, it was considered bad form to complain. Bruce was a perfectionist, but how he knew "perfection" when he saw it was a mystery beyond our collective comprehension. He left great songs off albums in place of only good ones that somehow better fit his conception of the record's thematic thrust.

The band had begun recording on April 3, 1979, starting off with a piece inspired by the Three-Mile Island accident four days earlier, though "Roulette" would not feature on any album for another nineteen years (though Springsteen did include it on a B-side of a single in response to fan complaints). The songs he did release would not be heard until *The River* appeared in October 1980. In the meantime, Springsteen scrapped one superb finished album called *The Ties That Bind* because he felt that it "wasn't personal enough" and "lacked the kind of unity and conceptual intensity" he desired. Eventually this notion, too, would be scrapped, in favor a of live-sounding, grab-bag approach. When they found a few spare minutes, Springsteen and Steve Van Zandt redis-covered and revived the career of veteran rocker Gary "U.S." Bonds, who had not had a hit since 1962. They met him singing in a hotel lounge, wrote him a few songs, booked some studio time, and then found a record company to release the album. "Dedication" was ter-rific, a perfect mixture of party and pathos. It cracked *Billboard*'s top thirty, and the Bruce-authored single "This Little Girl" made it to number eleven, giving Bonds his first hit song since the days of "Quarter to Three."

When *The River* was finally released, it expanded the concept of what a Bruce Springsteen song could be. Liv-ing alone on a farm in Holmdel, New Jersey, he had spent a lot of time watching old John Ford movies and American film noir. He discovered the music of Hank Williams, Roy Acuff, and early Johnny Cash, with a voice "so real and plain," it conveyed truths about the human heart revealed nowhere else. But he had also been listening to the records of a seventies rock band called the Raspberries, whose lush musical production and disposable pop melodies existed somewhere a planet apart from the work of Cash or Williams. *The River* does not try to choose among these various poles or to combine them, but simply embraces both. Songs like "Independence Day," "Point Blank," "Jackson Cage," and "Stolen Car" plunge into emotional depths similar to those explored in *Darkness*. Despite a fear of appearing "too entertaining," Springsteen also included a number of straight-ahead rockers like "Ramrod," "Crush on You," "Out in the Street," and "Cadillac Ranch," which has the infectious joy of a mindless Chuck Berry groove. He even threw in "Sherry Darling," which grew out of the great "Louie, Louie"–like "fraternity rock" songs of the early sixties, and "I Wanna Marry You" would have perfectly suited Ben E. King and the Drifters. The album's closer, "Wreck on the Highway," with its grizzled romantic fatalism, seems as if it could have been lost in the mail for forty years, when Hank Williams might have dropped it into a blue box somewhere in Montgomery, Alabama.*

Just as it does musically, the album refuses to choose between apparently contradictory emotional alternatives. Springsteen later said that during this period he was "attempting to pull myself into what I felt was going to be the adult world, so that when things became disorienting, I would be strong enough to hold my ground." The music helped, he said, because

---

*Actually, it was based on an old tune recorded in 1943 by Roy Acuff but written by Dorothy Dixon.

⌐ᴜᴋ has always been this joy, this certain happiness that is in its way the most beautiful thing in life. But rock is also about hardness and coldness and being alone. With *Darkness* it was hard for me to make those things coexist. . . . When I did *The River*, I tried to accept the fact that the world is a paradox, and that's the way it is. And the only thing you can do with a paradox is live with it.

According to Springsteen, the album's thematic unity derives from a Norman Mailer article that Bruce read, in which Mailer argues that "the one freedom that people want most is the one they can't have: the freedom from dread." If *Darkness* is, as Bruce has said, "about a guy stripping himself down, trying to find out where he stands [then] *The River* is about trying to get connected back with your relationship." Lyrically, the touchstones of Springsteen's work remained consistent: in twenty songs, there are thirteen "nights," ten "drives," nine "streets," and four "highways." But for the first time in his career, Springsteen also started writing traditional love songs like "I Wanna Marry You." During the recording of the album, Springsteen had attended the wedding of his sound engineer, an experience, he said, that "really got to me." He heard the rabbi explain that "when you're alone and without anybody, your dreams and fantasies are all of what you got, and that when you get married, when you get together with someone, that is the first step toward making those dreams a reality."

None of the songs on *The River* touch on specific contemporary culture or politics, but as Kit Rachlis pointed out, they conjure up "an American-provincial world of a guy, a girl, and a car, hurtling into the night, fleeing time itself." What did it mean, Stephen Holden asked, that the pop event of 1980 should be an album whose sound and substance resurrect the America of Eisenhower and Kennedy — a precountercultural, pre-Vietnam "promised land" where gasoline flows like water? Holden answered his own question: *The River* is about rock 'n' roll itself, Springsteen's "dictionary, encyclopedia and bible" of the music, and therefore of himself. "As one man's definition of rock 'n' roll classicism," Holden wrote, "*The River* makes emotional sense: the spirits of James Dean and Elvis merge in the body of a warmhearted hood from a backwater seashore town."

The River also yielded the artist's first top five single, "Hungry Heart." Springsteen, who reportedly did not want the song on the album, had originally planned to give it to the Ramones. It took Jon Landau to convince him that it would be OK to release such a radio-friendly song. The success of "Hungry Heart" was hardly a coincidence. As Steve Van Zandt, who coproduced the album, told journalist Fred Goodman: "I did a lot of things on that record to make sure it could be played on the radio." These included speeding up the recording and bringing in Mark Volman and Howard Kaylan of the Turtles to sing a Top 40 background vocal over uncommonly clean-sounding production. A few Springsteen purists cried "sellout," but Van Zandt insisted otherwise. "I knew it was the right time, the right song; it was not a compromise," he said. "It came out of his work." Indeed, the bouncy melody shelters a lyrical heart of darkness. A man decides to abandon his wife and family one day for reasons he can't explain; he just "went out for a ride" and "never went back." His explanation for his remarkably casual flight from his responsibilities? "Everybody's got a hungry heart / Everybody's got a hungry heart." The singer recognizes the feebleness of this justification, which is why he is trying to explain it to some "Jack" in a bar who is probably looking over his shoulder, trying to get away. And yet we sing along to the music on the radio, caught by a melodic hook as irresistible as any Beach Boy classic.

The River debuted at number four and hit number one two weeks later, with most critics agreeing that the hot, live sound of the album captures the excitement of the band like no recording before. Springsteen's audience had continued to grow throughout the previous year. Together with the E Street Band, he was voted Band of the Year by *Rolling Stone*'s critics, and Artist of the Year, Best Male Vocalist, and Best Songwriter by its readers. A two-hour NBC special titled "Heroes of Rock & Roll" broadcast that year ended with Bruce singing "Rosalita." When the New Jersey Meadowlands announced that Springsteen would be opening a new arena with six "homecoming" shows, it received 400,000 ticket requests, enough to fill the hall for more than twenty nights. When he played these dates, Springsteen was reportedly thrilled with the reception. "I couldn't hear the band," he said of the concerts. "I felt like we were the Beatles."

Meanwhile the sets got longer and longer. Steve Van Zandt told people that after the No Nukes event, he expected Bruce to make that show the basis for his regular act, like a normal rock concert. In fact, Springsteen simply added that ninety minutes to the two-hour show he already had, and then added even more. At a memorable New Year's 1981 show at Nassau Coliseum, they played thirty-eight songs in four and a half hours. Springsteen explained the incredible physical exertions of his performances in matter-of-fact terms: "If you start rationing, you're living your life bit by bit when you can live all at once. . . . That's what rock 'n' roll is: a promise, an oath. It's about being true to a particular moment." But he would also note, in later interviews, that part of what drove him was that he had little in the way of an emotional life off the stage.

At this point in time, Springsteen's only satisfying relationships, he would admit, were with the music, his band, and his fans. The band's lighting director, Marc Brickman, described these ties as "unrequited love," and told Fred Goodman, "Everyone, the whole band . . . just loved what this guy was doing so much and what he stood for and what he believed in by his songs that nothing else mattered. He never understood that. He never believed anybody loved him that much." Simon Frith has noted that the E Street Band, a group of highly skilled professionals, nevertheless managed to play every night with "a sort of amateurish enthusiasm, an affection for each other which is in sharp contrast to the bohemian contempt for their work (and their audience) which has been a strand of 'arty' rock shows since the Rolling Stones and the Doors. Springsteen's musicians stand for every bar and garage group that has ever got together in the fond hope of stardom."

Although Frith's analysis is ultimately critical, he correctly judges the character of the players. Springsteen openly depended on Clemons to heighten the show's dramatic tension and on Van Zandt to carry the band. Both musicians retained their idiosyncratic personalities — Clemons dressed like a pimp, and Van Zandt like a gypsy — and blended them into the collective entity. The E Street Band resembled nothing so much as the world champion 1969–70 New York Knicks, a team of first-rate players who achieved a greatness beyond each one's individual abilities through their willingness and ability to submerge their personal styles into a selfless whole.

It was his band that linked Bruce to the audience in a chain of imagined union that had no precedent in rock music and perhaps none in popular culture at all. Through the band, as Springsteen himself explained to Charlie Rose, he was able to "call up a sense of community and a sense of friendship" onstage. He considered it "an essential part" of what he communicated, allowing fans to invest themselves in the collective ideals it represented. To fans, Bruce allowed, the band symbolized the subject matter of the Springsteen canon: "trust, loyalty, friendship, community, the power of companionship."

Springsteen's take is accurate, but the communication of which he speaks often took place just below the surface, at almost a subconscious level. Beyond the songs and the performance itself, in that mix of talent, both spectacular and ordinary, flamboyant and understated, black and white, a young person could see his or her own ambitions reflected back with a sense of both shared struggle and celebration. A college friend once explained that the difference between Neil Young and Crazy Horse and Bruce Springsteen and the E Street Band was that the former made you feel as if they were really no better than you are, while the latter somehow convinces you that you can be as great as they are.

The intensity of these relationships, while perhaps not wholly emotionally satisfying for Bruce, continually reinvigorated his performance. Nervous on the opening of *The River* tour in Ann Arbor on October 3, 1980, Springsteen began the show with "Born to Run" but froze up and forgot the words. He thought, "Oh shit. I don't know these words. Not only do I not know these, I don't know any of the others. What the hell am I gonna do?" And then Bruce heard the audience singing, "In the days we sweat it out. . . ." "And it was great! And then it was fine." Even when no part of a song called for audience involvement, it was not unusual, many critics remarked, to see every person in the crowd mouthing all the words to every song.

On December 9, 1980, the night after John Lennon died, Steve Van Zandt was so distraught, he did not want to go onstage. Springsteen insisted that they owed it to John Lennon — and to their own fans — to play as planned. Before introducing "Born to Run," he told the mourning audience, "If it wasn't for John Lennon, a lot of us would be somewhere else tonight. It's a hard world that asks you to live with things that are unlivable, and it's hard to come out and play tonight, but there is nothing else to do." Fred Schruers would write of the show: "I've seen people digging firebreaks to save their homes, and I've seen some desperate fistfights, and, God knows, I've seen hundreds of rock 'n' roll shows, but I have never seen a human being exert himself the way Springsteen did that night in Philly."

After Lennon's death, Springsteen grew obsessed with his ability to defend both the authenticity of his artistic identity and the human being underneath it. "I want to be a rocker, a musician, not a rock 'n' roll star," he said at the time. He understood from the *Born to Run* experience that celebrity was both a trap and a distraction. Presley and Lennon aside, how could he ignore the death and destruction that seemed to accompany musical stardom in America as if it were an occupational hazard? "Burning out" or "fading away" appeared at times as if it might be the only escape offered. There were those who died and others, he noted in an interview, "who if they didn't die physically, they died essentially, just losing touch with everyone and everything that mattered." Think not only of Jimi, Janis, and Jim Morrison, but also Elvis, Sly Stone, Brian Jones, Miles Davis, Charlie Parker, and all the soul singers whose careers disappeared into alcohol, cocaine, and heroin addiction. The tally is astounding.

"The bigger you get, the more responsibility you have," Springsteen noted. "So you have to keep a constant vigilance. You got to keep your strength up, because if you lose it, then you're another jerk who's had his picture on the cover. A lot of guys lose it — that thing, that special thing they do — don't even know they've lost it and don't understand until they're affected afterward. Then they get angry." Springsteen had a clear understanding of just how easy it was to confuse the artist with the art, and he attempted whenever possible to play down those aspects of his public personality that did not relate specifically to his music. When a fan shouted, "I love you," at an October 1980 Oakland concert, Bruce shouted back into the darkness, "You don't even know me. You should see me at home."

Perhaps the most cherished "uncelebrity" story among Springsteen fans concerns the night in St. Louis when the band was off and Springsteen drove a rented car by himself to see the new Woody Allen film *Stardust Memories*. The 1980 release, Allen's most mean-spirited, is an astute but merciless attack on the emptiness of celebrity culture, which seems to place most of the blame on the star's fans, who are forever asking for autographs, offering unwanted opinions, and complaining that they liked his early, "funny" work best. How ironic, therefore, that Bruce would choose this night to spend time with a brave fan who approached him when the film was over to ask him if it rang true.

The guy took Bruce to his home somewhere deep in the suburbs, where they arrived a little after eleven. When they got home, his parents refused to believe it was really Bruce, so the kid had to run to his room, bring out an album, and hold it up next to Bruce's face. Bruce ate a two-hour late-night dinner with the whole family before the kid finally drove him back to his hotel. The most amazing aspect of this story is that it was Springsteen who considered himself fortunate. "I felt so good that night," he recalled. "Because here are these strange people I didn't know; they take you into their house, treat you fantastic. . . . You get somebody's whole life in three hours. And when I went back to the hotel I thought, 'What a thing to be able to do. What an experience to be able to have, to be able to step into some stranger's life.'" Springsteen even stayed friendly with the kid's mother, leaving tickets for her every time he returned to St. Louis for the next fifteen years.

It was about this time that critics first began wondering if Bruce Springsteen might not one day become bigger than the music itself — and what implications his presence might have for society at large. Following a typical 245-minute New York performance, John Rockwell speculated in the *New York Times* that Springsteen might represent "a future, not just of rock, but of the wider reaches of American culture." Rockwell found himself so moved by Springsteen's performance that he acknowledged it was "hard not to believe that he someday soon will make that next jump, staying true to rock's spirit, but bringing its message out beyond current limits of class, age and race — and in doing so help inspire the country as a whole in the ways already suggested in his music." Others professed to see in the Springsteen phenomenon a degree of slavish devotion that had the potential to mimic fascism. Stephen Fried wrote of watching Bruce do "one of his older tunes, standing on top of a speaker and raising his hand high in the air, one every other beat. The crowd followed along, as it did with almost everything else Springsteen did that night, and soon the Garden looked like a scene out of *Triumph of the Will*." Fried was quick to note that he would not assign any "insidious" motives to Springsteen but worried that he had already become "a god." "His concerts are less than rock shows and more like huge prayer meetings. Most of the people at the Garden wouldn't have known if Bruce had put on a good, bad or indifferent show. It was like the Pope in Philadelphia — who was going to say he prayed badly?"

Springsteen may have been considering these questions as well, for it was shortly after the end of the *River* tour that he decided he was not yet ready to be the world's biggest rock star. Politically, he was depressed and dispirited. Having traveled extensively in both the United States and Europe during the tour, he detected "an unhealthy sense of violence in the air on a daily basis" in the United States. He had money for the first time in his life, and he found it disorienting, as it threatened to separate him forever from the life he had lived until then as well as the body of work he had created. "First the car, the limousine . . . the big mansions on the hill," he explained in 1981. "I've always been suspicious of the whole package deal, and I'm scared of it. I'm afraid because you see so many people getting blown away, getting sucked down the drain." The stardom, moreover, felt like a threat to the authenticity of the identity he had worked so hard to protect. Having just turned thirty and suddenly finding that music alone was not enough, isolated and confused and approaching what he termed "rock bottom," he started to ask himself, "[What happens] when all the things I believed in when I was twenty-five break down? How do you live?" He realized he didn't know the answer.

Taking a house alone in Colt's Neck, New Jersey, after the tour, Springsteen asked his guitar tech for something suitable for "cheap and easy home recording." He ended up with a four-track Teac tape machine in his bedroom, and there, alone, Bruce Springsteen recorded his followup to *The River*. After completing the demo tape, he assembled the band and attempted to turn the songs into a rock 'n' roll album. But the record would not come. The ease of his unself-conscious voice was giving way, he worried, to the formality of the presentation and was destroying the essential nature of what he had been trying to accomplish. The songs needed what Springsteen termed "that austere, echoey sound, just the one guitar — one guy kinda telling his story." Finally Steve Van Zandt encouraged Springsteen to issue the demo itself. "It was a special moment," Van Zandt explained. "An artist could never get closer to his audience than this. Not because it was done with an acoustic guitar, but because he was literally singing for himself. It's the most direct, personal, accomplished artistic statement that you can make." Releasing the demo cassette on record turned out to be an enormous challenge until Chuck Plotkin finally solved the technical problems involved. The executives at Columbia were not thrilled to receive it, but they were given no choice. The company's president, Walter Yentikof, reportedly called it an album "you made in your garage, thank you. We'll do the best we can."

Nebraska, according to Springsteen, tells the story of people who are "isolated from their jobs, from their friends, from their family, from their fathers, mothers, not being connected to anything that's going on. . . . When you lose that sense of community, there's some spiritual sense of breakdown that occurs. You just get shot off somewhere where nothing really matters." For Bruce, the songs on the album are also connected to his early childhood, when his family was forced to live with his grandparents. He could smell the kerosene stove in the living room that was the source of heat for the entire house, and he recalled the power of the photograph of his father's sister, who had died at age five in an accident at the gas station around the corner: "Her ethereal presence from this 1920s portrait gave the room a feeling of being lost in time."

Nebraska feels as if it, too, is lost in time. Musically, it belongs to pre–rock 'n' roll America. Bryan Garman, writing in *Popular Music and Society*, tied the album to the history of the "hurt song": "Written in working-class language, hurt songs express the collective pain, suffering, and injustice working people have historically suffered, and articulate their collective hopes and dreams for a less oppressive future." By resurrecting the tradition of the hurt song, *Nebraska* not only gives voice to Springsteen's own battered psyche but also connects to a thread of social dislocation he sensed around him.

Consider the cultural and economic circumstances surrounding Springsteen's bedroom recording. The United States entered a deep recession in 1982, and many workers who saw their jobs go overseas felt an even more hopeless form of displacement than that experienced during the Depression. Unemployment reached 11 percent in 1982, but President Reagan still complained that he was tired of hearing about it every time someone lost his job in "South Succotash." In contrast to FDR, moreover, Reagan set out to destroy the union movement's power. Under his presidency, union membership dropped by 29 percent in the years leading up to the economic crisis, with the United Auto Workers alone seeing 250,000 workers lose their jobs. Those workers who remained unemployed grew increasingly quiescent, agreeing to corporate givebacks and less autonomy in the manufacturing process. An entire way of life — a way of life that had sustained the American Dream for generations — appeared to be crumbling.

If you wished to explore the lives of the people affected by these issues through American pop culture during this period, you had precious few options. There were plenty of songs about workingpeople in the ghetto of country music, but again, with the obvious exceptions of Willie Nelson, Johnny Cash, and a few others, they tended to be politically conservative or even reactionary. And they rarely attempted to address the contradictions of emotional life with any respect for the complexity of these emotions. While other rockers affected a concern for workingpeople — and many did so sincerely — these were, as John Mellencamp generously recognized, "footnotes to Springsteen," in terms of their cultural impact if not in the quality of their work. For outside of the music of Bruce Springsteen and perhaps a few other then-marginal artists — Richard Price and John Sayles come to mind — class remained the great unspoken subject of American life.

While writing *Nebraska*, Springsteen had been reading Flannery O'Connor, whose brilliant fiction frequently deals with grotesque, occasionally freakish characters, without ever mocking their longings. O'Connor had an uncanny ability to merge the deeply religious sensibility of her characters with the profane desires of their hearts in a gritty, personalized setting. These stories, Springsteen averred, reminded him of "the unknowability of God and contained a dark spirituality that resonated with my own feelings at the time." A second powerful influence on him during this period was a film he saw on television: Terrence Malick's *Badlands*, which tells the story of Charlie Starkweather and Caril Fugate and their 1958 killing spree across the Great Plains. Like a good Bruce Springsteen song, the film makes a seamless transition from the mundane details of the lives of inarticulate people to an epic commentary on inherent violence lurking in the banality of everyday life. Malick's characters, played by Martin Sheen and Sissy Spacek, seem wholly unconcerned with the moral consequences of their actions. Shooting innocents disturbs these two teenage runaways no more (or less) than Sheen's decision to shoot a football. Springsteen saw in the film a "stillness on the surface" that masked beneath it "a world of moral ambiguity and violence."

Musically, these notions swirled inside Springsteen's imagination and connected to his growing fascination with old-fashioned folk and country-and-western music. Having whetted his taste recording *The River*, Springsteen went deeper into the music, turning to the famous six-record *Anthology of American Folk Music* collected by the musical archivist Harry Smith and released on Moses Asch's Folkways label in 1952. The collection, released at the height of the McCarthy era, is an attempt by two left-wing bohemians to tell the story of another America, one that lived outside the mainstream of history and national politics. Both Asch and Smith were obsessed with the possibilities of political and cultural syncretism that folk music seemed to offer. Although the *Anthology*'s sales were small, its influence was enormous. It helped inspire the folk explosion of the early sixties, which in turn gave rock its social and intellectual edge. When Bob Dylan made history by plugging in an electric guitar at the 1965 Newport Folk Festival, horrifying his audience but redirecting the slow train of American popular culture, the song he chose was "Maggie's Farm," itself an homage to the Bently Boys' "Down on Penny's Farm," number twenty-five on the *Anthology*.

Though its cultural impact cannot be compared with Dylan's "going electric" at Newport, *Nebraska* nevertheless stands as a key moment in American cultural history. Virtually alone in the mass culture of the period, the record provides stark human testimony to the destruction of all forms of communal, psychological, and political support for workingpeople in Ronald Reagan's America. Like Dylan, Springsteen drew directly on Harry Smith's anthology. Song number seventy-four on the collection is a bluesy dirge called "Ninety-Nine-Year Blues" recorded by a North Carolina native named

Julius Daniels in February 1927. The song concerns a young black man who is arrested while visiting a new town under the "poor boy law." (In other words, he is guilty of being poor and black.) The judge sentences him to ninety-nine years in "Joe Brown's coal mine," and the injustice inspires the boy to express a desire to "kill everybody" in town.

Springsteen's response is "Johnny 99," which tells the story of a man named Ralph who loses his job when "they closed down the auto plant in Mahwah" and cannot find another. (Springsteen's songs may derive from the "hurt song" tradition, but they are grounded in the events of the day. In June 1980 Ford did close its twenty-five-year-old plant in Mahwah, New Jersey.) Facing foreclosure on his house, Ralph snaps, shoots a night clerk, and is charged with murder. When brought before Judge "Mean John Brown," Ralph does not try to shirk responsibility for what he's done, but he also notes that what drove him to the edge was a crisis not of his making. Told that he can expect to spend the rest of his life in prison, Ralph asks for the death penalty instead. There is no place in society for a man who cannot keep a job, feed his family, or maintain his dignity and the respect of his peers.

E. L. Doctorow has observed that whenever a novel features poor or working-class people as its protagonists, it is judged to be "political" and, therefore, not art. This is in part a comment on the prejudices of the critical elite in the United States, but it is also a reflection of the relative rarity, in recent years, of artistic attention paid to workingpeople. In November 1969 President Nixon gave a speech hailing the so-called silent majority — conservative Americans who disapproved of the increasing cultural liberalism of the youth culture, the entertainment industry, and the media world that surrounded them. The White House then secretly engineered tens of thousands of supportive telegrams in response, and newspapers and television stations were flooded with letters. The mainstream media discovered workingpeople as if for the first time. *Newsweek* professed to observe a "pendulum swing" back toward the silent majority in national politics and culture. *U.S. News* reported that "the common man is beginning to look like a Very Important Person indeed." *Time*'s editors concluded that "above all, Middle America is a state of mind."

As Barbara Ehrenreich demonstrates in her perceptive *Fear of Falling: The Inner Life of the Middle Class*, (1985), film and television writers also lavished considerable attention on blue-collar workers during this period, but it was attention of the most condescending kind. Two months after Nixon's election, CBS introduced us to the racist Archie Bunker and *All in the Family*. The hero of the film *Joe* (1970) complained: "The niggers are getting all the money. Why work? You tell me — why the fuck work when you can screw, have babies and get paid for it?" *Joe* was followed on the big screen by one working-class psychotic after another.

Taxi Driver's (1976) Travis Bickle was a crazy killer. In *Saturday Night Fever* (1977), working-class kids literally fall off the Brooklyn Bridge while fooling around; the romantic lead, John Travolta's Tony Manero, dreams of leaving these tawdry types behind and entering the world of glamour and romance in Manhattan. The three small-time workers/hoods in *Blue Collar* (1978) are out to rip off their union as it had done to them. The dumb working stiffs in *The Deer Hunter* (1979) draw guns against one another in a fight over hunting boots and eat their Twinkies with mustard. In the realm of popular art, to find blue-collar men speaking in a blue-collar language about blue-collar concerns, you had to go over to the turntable and put on a record by Bruce Springsteen.

Class was hardly a new subject for Springsteen, for even his early records are filled with young people yearning for escape into a better life. And certainly no one in a Bruce Springsteen song spoke college-educated English. With *Darkness*, however, the terms of the discourse began to change; characters now referred angrily to persons of authority ("Mister, I ain't a boy" in "Promised Land" or "Mister, when you're young" from "The River.") By *Nebraska*, virtually every song is addressed to the impersonal, unapproachable authority of a "mister," a "sir," a "judge," a "Mister State Trooper," or some combination thereof. The songs all take place in factories, mines, mills, convenience stores, kitchens, front porches, and VFW and union halls. But now decay infiltrates the workingman's life and refuges in the form of crime, drugs, and danger. Ralph gets into trouble at the Club Tip Top, located in a part of town "where when you hit a red light you don't stop."

What Springsteen accomplished with *Nebraska* was more than just forcing the subject of class into the mainstream cultural discourse. He also forged his own emotional confusion and political depression with his deepening mastery of literary and cinematic narrative. As Alan Rauch wrote in the journal *American Studies:* "Springsteen lets us hear the voice of someone who has been humbled far more than we have, even in the wide range of most of our experiences. . . . So intensely personal is the monologue of the narrator that it forces even the most sympathetic listener to step outside of the context of this monologue in order to see whether there are any valid connections with his or her own life." Nowhere is this power more evident than on the album's opening cut, "Nebraska," Charlie Starkweather's story told from the perspective of the mass murderer.

Springsteen does not falsely ennoble his working-class characters but humanizes them instead, demonstrating the complexity of their moral choices. For instance, the "good" brother in "Highway Patrolman," Joe Roberts, is forever trying to get the "bad" one, Frankie, out of trouble, even if it means bending the law a little. Joe is certainly the more socially responsible of the two, but he is also the one who received a farm deferment and married the girl they both loved. Frankie ended up in Vietnam and came back a lost soul. For Joe, who loves his fallen brother, "nothin' feels better than blood on blood." In "Used Cars," a young man walks down "the same dirty streets where I was born" as his father "sweats the same job from mornin' to morn." He is shamed by his father's inability to buy a new car, but the only hope of escape he himself can imagine is winning the lottery. In "Reason to Believe," a would-be groom stands alone, jilted and humiliated before his friends and family following a wedding ceremony that never took place. Still, he finds a "reason to believe" no more convincing, Springsteen avers, than that of a man poking a dead dog with a stick trying to make it run.

Released without much fanfare, critics nevertheless stood in awe of Springsteen's brave accomplishment. Mikal Gilmore writing in the *Los Angeles Herald Examiner*, called *Nebraska* "the most successful attempt at making a sizable statement about American life that popular music has yet produced." Greil Marcus observed that in Springsteen's portrayal of a society where "social and economic function have become the measure of all things and have dissolved all values beyond money and status," honest work becomes trivialized, honest goals reduced to a bet on the state lottery, and murder, however nihilistic, the only recognizable form of rebellion." Springsteen had fashioned "the most complete and probably the most convincing statement of resistance and refusal that Ronald Reagan's USA has elicited from any artist or politician."

Nebraska's message, however, was not one that great numbers of people wished to hear, and it was by far the worst seller of Springsteen's post–*Born to Run* career, appealing almost exclusively to hardcore fans. It was certainly not popular on the radio, and though Johnny Cash recorded fine versions of "Johnny 99" and "Highway Patrolman," his records were not selling well during this period, either. Springsteen did allow his first music video to be made to accompany the song "Atlantic City," but it was visually uninteresting and had little presence on MTV. As he chose not to tour in support of the record, if any possibility existed that Springsteen might one day take up John Rockwell's challenge and bring his message "beyond current limits of class, age and race — and in doing so help inspire the country as a whole," *Nebraska* was not going to be its occasion.

But far from swearing off electric guitars and amplifiers during this period, Springsteen had been popping up with surprising regularity at Jersey Shore clubs just to play loud rock 'n' roll with the local bands. As always, he had recorded far more songs for *Nebraska* than he could use, and was still experimenting with rock interpretations of them while simultaneously figuring out how to release *Nebraska*. One of the album's leftovers, "Born in the U.S.A.," told the story of an angry Vietnam veteran. When Bruce played it for Jon Landau, his manager thought it "a real odd thing, and it was not like anything else on the *Nebraska* album. And it was not like any other thing I've ever heard from Bruce — it sounded alien. It just didn't sound like it fit." Bruce himself was ambivalent, for it was one of his first songs about Vietnam, and he wanted to make certain he had the piece right. The two men agreed that it should be put aside for the time being; perhaps it might work out somehow on the next record.

You can't start a fire

You can't start a fire without a spark

— "Dancing in the Dark," 1984

A Working-Class Hero Is Something to Be

F. Scott Fitzgerald famously stated that there are no second acts in American life. In fact, for those with gambling hearts, America is one second act after another. When a second opportunity to ride the tidal wave of media megastardom came Bruce Springsteen's way in 1984, he was more than ready to claim it. "The *Born in the U.S.A.* experience obviously had its frightening moments," he later told an interviewer. "But I was thirty-five, and I had a real solid sense of myself by that time. I had a chance to relive my 1975 experience when I was calm and completely prepared, and went for it." By the time the experience was over, Springsteen would loom so large that, as Richard Ford described it, "he's become time, not the watch."

One of the strangest aspects of the *Born in the U.S.A.*

phenomenon was how serendipitous it appeared. True, *The River* had sold 3 million copies, but *Nebraska* had netted barely a fifth of that. Moreover, Springsteen was writing and recording *Born in the U.S.A.* and *Nebraska* simultaneously, the latter a series of dour Guthriesque lamentations that failed to reach beyond the most faithful fans, and the former a rousing, rock 'n' roll call to arms that captured the imagination of much of the Western world.

The release of *Born in the U.S.A.* repeated the now familiar pattern. The record was delayed interminably as Springsteen amassed his usual unmanageable assortment of songs — perhaps as many as a hundred this time. Inside the studio, according to Max Weinberg, the "bug" would often hit Springsteen after a night of recording had already been completed. Three new songs later, everyone would unpack their instruments, and recording would recommence, sometimes at five A.M.

Once again, Springsteen left off some of his greatest work — in this case, "Murder Incorporated," "Pink Cadillac," and "This Hard Land" — in favor of more generic material, for reasons that made sense only to him, and only for a brief moment. When the time came to finally release the record, Springsteen had worked himself into such a state of confusion that he invited the members of the band, the crew, and others to come in to the studio and vote for their favorites. "No Surrender," for instance, was an eleventh-hour decision based on heavy lobbying by Steve Van Zandt, though Springsteen thought it overly naive. "You don't hold out and triumph all the time in life," he averred. "You compromise, you suffer defeat, you slip into life's gray areas." But Van Zandt argued that "the portrait of friendship and the song's expression of the inspirational power of rock music was an important part of the picture," and Bruce capitulated. Springsteen may have been swayed by the fact that his friend and musical alter ego, with whom he had played since the days of Steel Mill, was finally leaving the band to follow his own muse. Van Zandt had participated in the early recording and production sessions for the record but was said to have clashed repeatedly with Landau about the direction of both.

Van Zandt's romanticism and loyalty to the band's roots had served Springsteen well for the previous decade, but it may no longer have been in sync with Springsteen's ambitions for the future. Springsteen had relied on Steve both as a friend and a confidante for nearly two decades. The song "Bobby Jean," in which Springsteen sings, "There ain't nobody nowhere nohow / gonna ever understand me the way you did," is commonly understood to be a tribute to their life friendship. So, to a considerable degree, is "No Surrender." Bruce stood up for Van Zandt at his wedding, which featured Little Richard officiating and Percy Sledge singing "When a Man Loves a Woman." But with *Nebraska* out of his system, he, too, was ready for the biggest of the big time. As he later explained, "My heroes, from Hank Williams to Frank Sinatra to Bob Dylan, were popular musicians. They had hits. There was a value in trying to connect with a large audience. It was a direct way you affected culture. It let you know how powerful and durable your music might be."

Landau himself was quick to recognize *Born in the U.S.A.*'s explosive commercial potential. The buzz inside the record company was sensational. Columbia assigned its top executive to oversee the album's marketing, and insiders were bandying about sales figures as high as 10 million. But when Springsteen thought he was finally finished, Landau objected: the record still needed an obvious hit single. He all but ordered Springsteen to go to his room and stay there until he wrote one. In an exchange that Landau later called "testy, by our standards," Bruce retorted, "You want another song, you write it yourself," but, of course, he wrote one anyway. "Dancing in the Dark" was an angry song about angst and alienation transformed into a synthesizer-heavy, disco-driven dance song. It turned out to be a smash, though Bruce felt that it "went as far in the direction of pop music as I wanted to go — and probably a little further."

Speaking of the single, Steve Van Zandt later said, "There would have been a big argument on that one if I'd have been there. I'm glad I wasn't." But by this time, Steve Van Zandt, who had rechristened himself "Little Steven" (following a brief interregnum as "Sugar Miami Steve"), had put together his own touring band, called the Disciples of Soul. The split was no doubt painful for both men. No one had been more important to Springsteen's success or better symbolized the band's neo-religious approach to rock 'n' roll. Steve Van Zandt, Fred Goodman argued in 1997, "wants the band the way no one else wants the band. . . . He invests it with a certain meaning and drive." According to Goodman, Steve once talked Bruce out of billing the show as Bruce Springsteen *with* the E Street Band as opposed to Bruce Springsteen *and* the E Street Band. He grabbed Bruce and said, "That's wrong. You're the lead singer of the E Street Band. . . . You're in the band." And it was this romantic view of Bruce and the band that apparently clashed with Landau and Columbia. "You can make a very good living — a very good living — selling a couple of million records and selling out arenas," Steve argued. "I don't think we needed to be any more successful."

With all these competing pressures, the album came out a jumble. It is Springsteen's most melodic album, recorded virtually live, but it lacks the literary and thematic coherence of his past decade's work. "Cover Me" had been written for Donna Summer but was pulled back when the demo sounded too good to give away. "Darlington County" was a *Darkness* outtake. "I'm on Fire" grew out of a Johnny Cash/Tennessee Three rhythm track Springsteen liked. "Downbound Train," "My Hometown," and "Born in the U.S.A." were all considered for *Nebraska.* They are all good songs, and a few are nearly great, but the record is not a great *album* in the sense that *Born to Run, Darkness,* or *Nebraska* are. While Springsteen acknowledged that he had grown "pretty tired of writing lyrics about cars and highways" and wanted to "move on," he did not yet have a clear destination in mind. He later admitted, "I was not satisfied with the *Born in the U.S.A.* record. I did not think I made all the connections I wanted to make."

But commercially, Springsteen made one of the biggest connections any artist has ever made, and *Born in the U.S.A.* quickly became Columbia's biggest-selling record ever. More important, the album's success opened a window that finally, in John Rockwell's words, allowed Springsteen to address "the wider reaches of American culture" and "help inspire the country as a whole." *New York Times* music critic Stephen Holden cheered him as "one of a very small number of rock performers who uses rock to express an ongoing epic vision of this country, individual social roots and the possibility of heroic self-creation." With *Born in the U.S.A.*, he argued, Springsteen had "transfused rock and roll and social realism into one another," while "the compassion and the surging brawn of his music makes his very despairing vision of American life into a kind of celebration."

Whether *Born in the U.S.A.* represents a despairing or celebratory vision of the United States would ultimately become a question of considerable political significance. As Springsteen's success grew, he soon became a multilayered symbol to millions of people, as well as a pawn in the country's ongoing culture wars. Whether because of or in spite of the actual content of the music, few living artists of any kind have ever seen their work exercise the power and influence exhibited by *Born in the U.S.A.* in 1980s popular and political culture. For a brief historical moment, Bruce Springsteen became, in Richard Ford's memorable phrase, "a small, well-intentioned, mass movement."

The frenzy began almost instantaneously. The album went platinum within forty-eight hours of its release and triple-platinum shortly thereafter. It owned the number one spot not only in the United States and Canada but also in Britain, West Germany, and the Netherlands. *Born in the U.S.A.* eventually yielded seven top-ten singles and remained on *Billboard*'s charts for two full years. Though such numbers are often inflated, at last count its sales were said to be approaching 18 million in the United States and perhaps 24 million worldwide. The mere mention of a Bruce Springsteen concert during this period was enough to upset local traffic patterns and phone service. And the wave grew larger and larger. At the beginning of the tour, the Meadowlands sold out ten shows — 202,027 tickets — in two days. By the following summer such numbers would seem almost sluggish in comparison.

In the summer of 1985, after an American arena tour and a European tour that played to crowds as large as seventy thousand people, Springsteen and the band came home to make the final move into outdoor football stadiums. That's when the fun really began. Every time tickets went on sale in some major stadium, the phone company had to brace for a local emergency. In Chicago, Illinois Bell put its tornado computer program into effect. In Washington, D.C., ticket requests played havoc with the Pentagon and the White House phone systems. But even the stadiums were not large enough to satisfy demand. Springsteen played to 330,000 people in four shows in L.A. When he returned to Jersey, he sold out 236,000 tickets in a day, added two more shows, and quickly sold those out, bringing the total to roughly 360,000, nearly equal to the number of people who attended the original Woodstock festival.

Although prices were kept relatively low — the Jacksons were charging thirty dollars for their Victory tour while Springsteen was asking only sixteen dollars for a show that lasted three times as long — the tour was still extraordinarily lucrative. With 155 shows, including 28 outdoor stadiums in North America, ticket sales alone amounted to a reported $117 million, with another thirty or so million added in for merchandising. Include the royalties from tens of millions of records sold, and the young man who so impressed John Hammond with his nonchalance about money earned more in the period 1984–86 than some developing countries. "We started out as a band," Danny Federici later noted, "[and] turned into a super, giant corporate moneymaking machine."

Critics loved the new record as most of them had loved every Springsteen record since *Born to Run*, and the stage show even more so. The *Los Angeles Herald*

Examiner's Mikal Gilmore was hardly alone in admitting that when he saw Bruce Springsteen perform, he found "the kind of fulfillment and community that only the best friendships and kinships might bring one, which is to say, I see an oath of love and meaning played out with full heart." Such personal declarations from otherwise tough-minded writers were the norm, rather than the exception in the days when the E Street Band ruled the musical planet.

Springsteen's multifaceted achievement at this point in his career may be unique in the history of American popular music. Elvis was a great singer and charismatic performer; but he was no writer, much less thinker. The same is true of Frank Sinatra. Bob Dylan was a powerful poet with immeasurable influence on the culture of the sixties and early seventies, but his records never sold a fraction of the number racked up by *Born in the U.S.A.*, and much of his later work proved indecipherable. Michael Jackson's *Thriller* topped Springsteen on sales alone, but his lyrics seldom had any depth. But Bruce Springsteen was everything at once: a hugely popular performer, a thoughtful poet, and a potent political/cultural force. At the end of 1984 Springsteen and the band easily swept *Rolling Stone*'s readers' and critics' polls. From the readers they received Artist of the Year, Band of the Year, Male Vocalist of the Year, Producer of the Year, Album of the Year, and Single of the Year. From the critics, second place for Artist of the Year, and first for Band of the Year, Songwriter of the Year, and Album of the Year. While Jackson, Prince, or Madonna might have rivaled Springsteen during those years in sales numbers, no popular artist since the Beatles had ever achieved this combination of mass popularity and critical acclaim.

How did it happen? Part of the reaction was no doubt the result of the creation of a more media-friendly Bruce Springsteen. Following *Nebraska*, the artist who now presented himself to the marketplace was, cosmetically, a new man. Physically, Springsteen had transformed himself. Gone was the scrawny, leather-jacketed street punk with the poor complexion, bad teeth, and even worse hair. Having hired a personal trainer, Springsteen emerged from the *Born in the U.S.A.* sessions with biceps bulging. The new macho Bruce also had his teeth fixed, banished the three gold rings from his ear, discovered a competent barber to do something with his curly locks, and stocked up on a few dozen pairs of perfectly stonewashed, extremely tight pairs of Levi jeans. (Sales of the pants increased precipitously during this period, which *Time* noted under the headline PANTING FOR BRUCE'S JEANS.) Overnight, the Jersey rat had become an all-American sex symbol.

This transformation was particularly striking in the Brian De Palma–directed video of "Dancing in the Dark," released to promote the new album. Having interrupted the opening show of his tour to perform the song twice in a row for the cameras, a preppy-looking, clean-shaven Bruce Springsteen lip-synched his lyrics, and mugged on stage with Courtney Cox. Sam Hughes, the teenage protagonist of Bobbie Ann Mason's 1985 novel *In Country*, sees the video and observes, "His jeans were as tight as rubber gloves, and he danced like a revved-up sports car about to take off." She dreams of being pulled out of the audience for a dance, à la Ms. Cox, "And he would pull her out of the front row and dance with her in the dark."

The sunny new Springsteen is also evident in the album's packaging. Gone are the blank existentialist stares of the Frank Stefanko photographs for *Darkness* and *The River* and the stark, depressing Robert Frank–style artwork of *Nebraska*. This time Springsteen receives the full Annie Leibowitz celebrity treatment. The cover features Bruce's newly tightened rear end posed before a waving American flag. Promotional photos placed the singer in front of the same flag, but this time, staring directly into the camera, his expression, in Timothy White's felicitous phrase, "like a puckish Patton." The band, too, looks cleaned up and scrubbed down for the MTV generation. The elfin Nils Lofgren replaced the scruffy gypsy Van Zandt on guitar, and pretty Patti Scialfa had joined to help the boys hit the high notes.

But looks alone do not move units. The disjoint between the new made-over Bruce and his uncompromising material was also reflected in the record itself. For all its thematic weaknesses, however, *Born in the U.S.A.* is still a great rock record. Robert Christgau, the dean of the rock-crit intelligentsia, found the album to be "an

amazing feat . . . on singing and songwriting alone."
Christgau credited Landau and Springsteen's "crazed
perfectionism" and "techno-hubris" with the creation of
a record with "ringing live intensity," "joyous release,"
and "honest laughs." Indeed, from the opening beats of
Weinberg's drum on the title cut, through the last organ
riffs of "My Hometown," the record delivers a succession of perfect pop moments. What philosophical complexity it offers derives not from the melodies or the
lyrics themselves but from the frequent conflict between the two. Song after song features a thrilling rave-
up about a miserable human being. In what must be
a record — or perhaps a backhanded tribute to Sam
Cooke — fully a quarter of the songs on the album are
sung by, or about, members of road gangs. "Glory Days"
features a character so pathetic he has to appropriate
other people's high school victories, having none of his
own to stoke his nostalgia. "I'm on Fire" involves a protagonist whose infatuation is so obsessive, he might be
dangerous. Just about the only song in which form and
content seem matched is the dirgelike "My Hometown," which really belonged on *Nebraska.*

Nowhere does the record's lyric-melodic confusion
manifest itself with greater consequence than on its title
track. Lyrically, the song is as straightforward as any
Springsteen had ever recorded. A young man is "born
down in a dead man's town" and takes his first kick
when he "hit the ground." He finds himself in "a little
hometown jam" and instead of going to jail, is sent to

Vietnam "to go and kill the yellow man." His brother is killed at Khe Sahn, leaving a Vietnamese loved one behind. And when the young man finally returns, he finds he has lost his job. The song's final verse is a cry of anguish:

> *Down in the shadow of the penitentiary*
> *Out by the gas fires of the refinery*
> *I'm ten years burning down the road*
> *Nowhere to run, ain't got nowhere to go*

Nothing in this lyric can credibly be interpreted as optimistic, much less celebratory of life in the United States. To be born in the U.S.A. is a curse for its hero, a cross to bear, not cause for a rousing cheer. Springsteen said he wrote the song about a man who "wants to strip away that mythic America which was Reagan's image of America. He wants to find something real, and connecting. He's looking for a home in his country." If he had included the song on *Nebraska*, as originally planned, few listeners would have been confused about its meaning. But when he took it into the studio to try it out with the band, lightning struck during the second complete take. As Mark Hagan described it, "Weinberg's nuclear snare drum, Bittan's trumpet voluntary of a synthesizer lick, the whole band's rolling fanfare for the common soldier all came tumbling out in one mighty ocean wave which rolled on into the unplanned ninety seconds of instrumental outro thundering to fade." Springsteen's vocals, Timothy White noted, "were gravelly bursts . . . like a souped-up Chevy skidding away from the soft shoulder on the road." Weinberg called the session "the greatest single experience I've ever had recording." Landau modestly termed it "the most exciting thing that ever happened in a recording studio."

Springsteen would later admit that while his acoustic version might have communicated the song's message more aptly, the band's version was the song's "most powerful presentation." Had he tried to "undercut or change the music," he "would have had a record that might have been more easily understood, but not as good."

Unfortunately, millions of people heard the band version with exactly the opposite message of what Springsteen intended. For many, the music's visceral power made the lyrics seem beside the point. And when Springsteen unfurled an enormous American flag as he sang the song in concert, the anger of the lyrics became further obscured by the patriotic symbolism that surrounded it. Attending a Springsteen concert at the Capitol Center in Landover, Maryland, in September 1984, the right-wing pundit George Will perceived in "Born in the U.S.A.," "a grand, cheerful affirmation" of American life. As he reported in his column in more than a thousand newspapers a few mornings later: "I have not got a clue about Springsteen's politics, if any, but flags get waved at his concerts while he sings songs about hard times." As if trying to win simultaneous

Pulitzers in the categories of ignorance and chutzpah, he then went on to use Springsteen's anthem to bash American workers. "If all Americans made their products with as much energy and confidence as Springsteen and his merry band make music," he insisted, our economy would not suffer from so many "slipshod products."

Ronald Reagan's image makers read Will's column that morning and came up with a brilliant idea: Why not draft Springsteen into the president's reelection campaign? If they could not obtain Bruce in person, they could certainly hijack his persona. Five days after Will's piece appeared, President Reagan officially announced his candidacy in New Jersey against the backdrop of the Statue of Liberty. "America's future" explained the president, "rests in a thousand dreams inside our hearts; it rests in the message of hope in songs of a man so many young Americans admire: New Jersey's own Bruce Springsteen. And helping you make your dreams come true is what this job of mine is all about." New Jersey senator Bill Bradley also jumped into game, authoring a page-one opinion piece in *USA Today* in which he discerned in Springsteen the message "Forget that the factory closed or that the marriage broke up" and simply "let the good times roll." (Springsteen later commented, ruefully, though not quite accurately, "If the song was misunderstood, it was only misunderstood by Republicans.") It was only a matter of time before Chrysler decided it would be a good idea to offer Springsteen $12 million to use "Born in the U.S.A." in a car commercial.* But as Springsteen had already explained in a 1984 interview, "Independence is nice. That's why I started this. For the independence. I'm telling my story out there. I'm not telling anybody else's. I'm saying what I want to say. That's the only thing I'm selling."

Politicians were not the only ones who went too far in reinterpreting the new Bruce Springsteen. In the media he was further transformed into a made-for-TV version of himself — an image not unlike that he projected in the "Dancing in the Dark" video. A *People* magazine writer attended one show and found "a hearty, all-American air to the proceedings that one doesn't usually find at this sort of event." *Newsweek*, offering Bruce its second cover (this time with no interview at all), could not resist placing Springsteen in its pantheon of all-American heroes and described him as "rock 'n' roll's Gary Cooper — a simple man who expresses strong beliefs with passion and unquestioned sincerity." One sentence later, however, Bruce was "rock 'n' roll's Jimmy Cagney . . . streetwise and fiery, a galvanic mixture of body and soul." Perhaps the most honest account of the source of Springsteen's astonishing popularity came from *McCall's*. In its article "Bruce Springsteen: Why

* This comedy of errors recalled an earlier Springsteen-related political farce. In 1980 the New Jersey state legislature came within one vote of naming "Born to Run" the state's official anthem, until someone realized that much of what Bruce and Wendy were running from was, in fact, New Jersey.

He Makes Us Feel Good," one interviewee answered sweetly and simply: "Bruce has great buns."

It is a complicated and ultimately unanswerable question as to just how much of the responsibility for these interpretations can be attributed to Springsteen himself. But among some leftist critics, as well as Springsteen haters of all stripes, the answer was, pretty much all of it. They professed to see in Springsteen and his manager's machinations a manipulative attempt to embrace the symbolism and underlying ethos of Reaganism while dancing delicately away from its reactionary foundation.

According to this line of argument, virtually every political action Springsteen took during this period was actually part of a cynical media strategy. *Esquire* published a piece by a writer named John Lombardi that was typical of this approach. "Ten years after Schwarzenegger, he'd pumped so much iron he practically clanked, and opened 'Born in the U.S.A.' against a monolithic American flag motif. This was consonant with the peaking of the fitness craze, with Reagan's huge plurality in the presidential election." The author quoted one "insider" who argued that "pop stars at that level are like surfers. They pick a wave and try to ride it to the beach. In '84, the wave was Vietnam veterans, unions, and food banks. No other pop star had defined his image in that 'populist' way." In his 1999 study, *Flowers in the Dustbin*, Jim Miller offers up a more sophisticated version of this interpretation, in which Springsteen's public image became a "fetishized" commodity, a "prefab" token of a "rapturous transcendence, producing a variety of goods that could be purchased and (for the truly idolatrous) reverently collected." According to Miller, this ended "the age of innocence in rock and roll . . . probably forever."

Whether these arguments had any factual basis only Springsteen and Landau can answer. But even if they held some truth, the assumptions that lay beneath them remain problematic. For one, they assume nearly Svengali-like abilities on the part of the two men to manipulate the global marketplace. Second, they treat the audience as if it were composed almost exclusively of buffoons. Third, they ignore the complexity of the interplay between the communicator and communicatee, as well as the role that market forces play in distorting and perverting what both sides hear when the communication is taking place. By the time of "Born in the U.S.A.," Anthony DeCurtis observed, "marketing — the creation and the selling of an image — became an essential component of an artist's success. Videos, video compilations, long-form videos, corporate sponsorships, product endorsements, T-shirts, book deals, interviews, television appearances, movie tie-ins, songs for soundtracks — all that began to envelop what was considered a rebel's world."

Regarding the frequent misinterpretation of "Born in the U.S.A.," Springsteen himself complained, "It's not that people aren't taught to think, it's that they aren't taught to think hard enough. I mean, 'Born in the U.S.A.' is not ambiguous. You just have to listen to the verses." But perhaps that protest is a bit naive; the misinterpretation and mishearing of rock lyrics is a time-honored tradition. While performers often like to believe that they are imparting subversive or even revolutionary messages to their audiences, in fact, the reverse is more likely the case. According to a major study by R. Serge Denisoff, most listeners hear protest songs as pure entertainment rather than as documents of political resistance or social significance.

Much of the criticism that charges Springsteen with reinforcing the principles of Reaganism ignores, at the very least, the manner in which "Born in the U.S.A." served in the mid-eighties as a foundation upon which to make a stand against those same principles. While Springsteen's politics were hardly revolutionary, they did run very much against the grain of mainstream culture. They had nothing in common with the full frontal attacks on Amerikkka that emanated from sixties bands like the Jefferson Airplane, Country Joe and the Fish, or the (pre–Jon Landau) MC5. Living in central Jersey and declared 4-F for the draft, Springsteen basically missed the sixties, save for the hair. His politics derived, instead, from ground zero of the 1950s American Dream. His touchstones were cars, girls, buddies, and romance. He had absorbed all of television's Horatio Alger allegories about hard work and having it all. He idealized the mutual-support networks of small-town communities. But he found, as Ray Pratt noted, that *"it doesn't work; it's lethal.* It grinds you down, it engenders 'dreams that tear you apart,' it delivers a promise that is not just a lie but something worse. And that something gnaws at one, it is a promise so arresting and seductive that you get trapped only to explode into flight or violence."

Before the *Born in the U.S.A.* tour, Springsteen had demonstrated considerable unease whenever asked to speak politically. During No Nukes in 1979, he made no statement about the subject of nuclear power and chose not to play what would have been his most appropriate song, "Roulette," written about the Three-Mile Island scare. He said nothing in 1982 when he joined Jackson Browne again, for a rendition of "The Promised Land" at a nuclear-freeze rally in New York's Central Park. His first tentative political comments, oddly enough, came during the European leg of *The River* tour, when he explained to a Parisian audience that he had recently been reading Henry Steele Commager and Allan Nevins's *A Pocket History of the United States.* First published in 1942, the book is a typical "progressive" interpretation of American history for that period, though it is more eloquent than most. Written during World War II, its authors focus on the nation's struggle for freedom and tolerance.

In Springsteen's original reading of the work, he discovered that things weren't the way they were meant to be — like the way my old man was living, and his old man and the life that was waiting for me — that wasn't the original idea. But even if you find those things out, it's so hard to change those things. It wasn't until I started listening to the radio and I heard something in those singers' voices that said there was more to life than what my old man was doing and the life that I was living. And they held out a promise, and it was a promise that gets broken every day in the most violent way. But it's a promise that never ever dies, and it's always inside of you.

Somehow Springsteen discovered rock 'n' roll in progressive history and vice versa. Like many self-educated people, Springsteen was less comfortable discussing ideas and ideologies than speaking in purely "human" terms. His politics were intensely personal and derived from his understanding of how given individuals react to certain situations. In this regard, he shared a great deal with Ronald Reagan, in his willingness to generalize and make larger political points from specific situations. The song "Born in the U.S.A." is the story of one man, but step back a few feet, and you can see that it actually tells the story of thousands.

In the summers of 1984 and 1985, Springsteen took the first steps of putting himself forth as a catalyst to translate the individual "troubles" about which he had always written into political and social issues that engaged larger groups of people. He was, in his own words, "tryin' to figure out where do the aesthetic issues that you write about intersect with some sort of concrete action, some direct involvement, in the communities that your audience comes from?"

A few years earlier, Springsteen had happened upon a copy of Ron Kovic's harrowing Vietnam memoir, *Born on the Fourth of July*. Through the story of this one young man's own disillusionment, Springsteen came to understand the mistreatment of the boys of his own generation who had been sent to Vietnam and then abandoned at home. After meeting Kovic and later Bobby Muller, founder of Vietnam Veterans of America, he agreed to perform a benefit for the organization. The concert, called A Night for the Vietnam Veteran, took place in Los Angeles in August 1981.

The show raised $100,000 for the veterans' organization and for the L.A. mental health clinic that specializes in veterans' care. Muller has credited Springsteen with saving the organization and beginning the process through which Vietnam vets finally became reconciled to the country that had so mistreated them. Shortly thereafter, Springsteen began speaking more and more about his generation's experience of Vietnam, and would often tell the story of how the drummer of his first band, the Castiles, had been killed in the war. Springsteen went on to write some of his best material about Vietnam vets and their efforts to reintegrate themselves into society ("Highway Patrolman," and "Shut Out the Light") and, in doing so, helped these efforts bear fruit. The entire experience was clearly a powerful one for

Springsteen, and he began to look for ways to expand upon it. Rejecting the solutions of traditional politics, he told Kurt Loder, "I want to try and just work more directly with people; try to find some way [to] tie into the communities we come into." Beginning with the *Born in the U.S.A.* tour, Springsteen set up a program whereby his organization would pick out a local group — usually a food bank — that took care of people in need. He would mention the work they did from the stage and encourage audience members to do their part for the cause. Springsteen's own donations — $10,000 during the arena portion of the tour and $25,000 during the stadium portion — also inspired considerable debate. On the one hand these amounts of money were negligible to Springsteen, given the tens of millions he was then earning. On the other, they represented considerably more than any rock star of remotely comparable stature was contributing at that time. The gesture was intended, his defenders insisted, to inspire others to action, rather than provide a solution by itself.

Ultimately, Springsteen's views were those of an old-fashioned New Deal social democrat; his gifts as an artist lay in his ability to articulate a simple vision of social decency. Even so, Bruce never saw himself as a crusader but viewed this phase of his career as a simple recognition of his civic responsibility. "The thing that frightened me most was seeing all that waste . . . people's lives wasted. . . . It seemed like if you're a citizen, and you're living here, then it's your turn to take out the garbage." What motivated his vision was the honorable ideal of another America: an America he imagined where workingpeople were treated with respect and where community members banded together to help one another in hard times.

But Springsteen was a poet, not a politician. He didn't have a program; he had a feeling — that, and the greatest rock and roll band on the planet. And using the power of that band, and the microphone that *Born in the U.S.A.* placed in his hands, he did his best to empower a tradition that had been buried beneath a sea of laissez-faire ideology and chauvinistic propaganda.

If Springsteen made certain compromises, both personal and musical, to achieve this level of communication, he never abandoned the core values he had always sought to communicate. Whatever confusion existed about his motives was due to some degree to these compromises rather than the inherent contradiction between the medium and the message. Springsteen was an individualist speaking through the voice of a corporate-dominated delivery system, an artist who employed an essentially conservative set of symbols to deliver a message of personal liberation and communal responsibility. Because, Frank McConell observed, Springsteen "is so deeply encased in, surrounded by the culture of rock, he can do what no rock singer has done before: raise it to the level of metaphor." "Hey ho, rock and roll deliver me from nowhere," Springsteen sings with so profound a lack of irony that his message is nearly impossible to give credence to in a postmodern universe. And he himself so clearly believes in it — and fights so hard to keep believing it — that he somehow makes his audience believe it, too.

In the late autumn of 1986, Springsteen finally released the extended live album for which fans had been clamoring for more than a decade. At some stores demand was so high, it was literally sold off the back of trucks, as it proved impossible to get it onto the shelves without disrupting the long lines that formed around the block. The five-record set commanded the largest advance orders of any album in history. It sold a million copies in its first five days, grossing $50 million and earning Springsteen $7.5 million during the first week it was released. By the end of the year it had sold roughly 3.5 million "units," with gross revenue estimated at $45 million. Bruce Springsteen was now one of the richest men in America and also its most prominent spokesperson for the dignity of the worker and the culture of egalitarianism. It was a tricky row to hoe, and in the future its contradictions would inform Springsteen's music, adding to its complexity and self-examination.

Many Springsteen fans anguished during this period that their intimacy with the artist who had meant so much to them for so many years would now be gone forever. Springsteen concerts had become huge events, and the members of the invisible church of Springsteen felt themselves being shunted aside — and occasionally crushed — by millions of loudmouthed parvenus who insisted on screaming during all the wrong parts of the songs, would go to the bathroom during "Johnny 99," and still missed the point of "Born in the U.S.A." I remember sitting at the top of Giants Stadium, thinking about the first time I had seen Springsteen, nine years earlier in a hall one-twentieth the size. I had wondered back then what the world would be like if Bruce were the biggest rock star on the planet, and now I knew: it was in many ways the same as it had always been — only tickets were a lot more difficult to come by, and Bruce was harder to see. But I had to admit to myself that the shows had lost a bit of their magic. With the move into stadiums, Springsteen was forced to sacrifice virtually all the subtlety and spontaneity his performances once offered. To add insult to injury, Springsteen even married a model — just like Billy Joel — and moved to L.A. What was next? An album of duets with Julio Iglesias?

Given the heights to which he had risen by this time, one would have guessed that Bruce Springsteen was being set up for an equally spectacular fall; those whom the gods destroy they first deliver six nights of sellout crowds at Giants Stadium. In fact, he lived through the experience of cultural deification and came out the other side pretty much as he had gone in. At his induction into the Rock and Roll Hall of Fame in 1999, Springsteen was introduced by U2's Bono with the bemused observation:

He hasn't done the things most rock stars do. He got rich and famous, but never embarrassed himself with all that success, did he? No drug busts, no blood changes in Switzerland. Even more remarkable, no golfing! No bad hair period, even in the eighties. No wearing of dresses in videos. No embarrassing movie roles, no pet snakes, no monkeys. No exhibitions of his own paintings. No public brawling or setting himself on fire. . . . Rock stars are supposed to make soap operas of their lives, aren't they? If they don't kill themselves first. Well, you can't be a big legend and not be dysfunctional. It's not allowed.

Springsteen, as Bono smartly explained, took his work too seriously for all that. "He didn't buy the mythology that screwed so many people. Instead, he created an alternative mythology, one where ordinary lives became extraordinary and heroic."

Something in Bruce Springsteen was firmly anchored in the person he had been rather than in the one the world wanted him to become. He had learned, ten years earlier during the *Born to Run* hysteria, that fame and celebrity were, beyond a certain point, a distraction and a distancing mechanism that interfered with his ability to accomplish the goals he set for himself. "If the price of fame is that you have to be isolated from the people you write for, then that's too fucking high a price to pay," he told an interviewer. And Bruce Springsteen knew better than anyone, "you just can't walk away from the price you pay."

When you're alone you're alone

When you're alone you're alone

When you're alone you're alone

When you're alone you ain't nothing but alone

— "When You're Alone," 1987

God Have Mercy on the Man
Who Doubts What He's Sure Of

B y the time he finished the 155 shows of the *Born in the U.S.A.* tour, Bruce Springsteen had become an inescapable icon in American culture. The *Born in the U.S.A.* image had been appropriated to advertise L&M cigarettes, Citicorp checking accounts, Casio synthesizers, Koss headphones, and even VISTA volunteer internships. Unable to secure rights to the original, Chrysler launched an ad campaign titled "The Pride Is Back: Born in America." Miller beer pronounced itself "Born and Bred in the USA." The United Way sought donations with full-page advertisements announcing, "This Is Your Hometown." A skin-trade entrepreneur even jumped on the bandwagon with the enduring cinematic classic *Porn in the USA*.

Springsteen's generosity with the songs he wrote but

didn't record also had the effect of extending his artistic influence. The range of styles to which his music proved adaptable ensured that almost no category of pop music — from disco, through country and western, to punk — did not feature at least one Bruce Springsteen hit. Many first-rate novelists, including Bobbie Ann Mason, Richard Ford, Stephen King, and T. C. Boyle, also found inspiration in Springsteen's work and created characters and stories inspired by his images and lyrics.

Springsteen's most famous — albeit uncredited — contribution to film culture had come a decade earlier, via Martin Scorsese and Robert De Niro. The pair was filming *Taxi Driver* when De Niro happened to join the rest of the celebrity set to see the *Born to Run* sensation at the Roxy in L.A. When, at the end of the show, the audience screamed for more, Springsteen looked back in mock confusion and screamed, "Are you talkin' ta me?" By the process of creative osmosis, the line made it into De Niro's famous ad-libbed mirror monologue and became a seventies cultural signifier. The De Niro hijacking was a fluke, no doubt, but Springsteen's cinematic style of songwriting continued to appeal to numerous filmmakers. The best of his songs have all the tension and complexity of great short fiction, John Sayles has noted. "'Jungleland' and 'Meeting Across the River' pack as much punch in a few minutes as I got into *City of Hope*, which is a whole movie." Remarkably diverse filmmakers have either used existing Springsteen songs in their films or asked Bruce if he wouldn't mind writing them a new one: Sayles's *Baby It's You* (1983) and *Limbo* (1999), Paul Schrader's *Light of Day* (1987), Norman Jewison's *In Country* (1989), Richard Pearce's *Leap of Faith* (1992), Kenneth Branagh's *Peter's Friends* (1992), Paul Brickman's *Risky Business* (1983), Michael Moore's *Roger & Me* (1989), David Zucker's *Ruthless People* (1986), Peter Bogdanovich's *Texasville* (1990), Barry Levinson's *Tin Men* (1987), Brian De Palma's *Wise Guys* (1986), Adam Sandler's *The Wedding Singer* (1998), John Duigan's *Lawn Dogs* (1998), Kevin Reynolds's *187* (1997), Jonathan Demme's *Philadelphia* (1993), Barbara Kopple's *American Dream* (1990), Tim Robbins's *Dead Man Walking* (1995), Cameron Crowe's *Jerry Maguire* (1996), James Mangold's *CopLand* (1997), and Sean Penn's *The Crossing Guard* (1994). Three years earlier, Penn directed his first movie, *The Indian Runner*, which includes no Springsteen music but whose plot is nothing more than *Nebraska*'s "Highway Patrolman" given flesh and blood.

Springsteen also inspired a particularly devoted and energetic following among comedians and comic impersonators. Among the best of these was a single put out in 1982 by a Baltimore cartoonist named Tom Chalkley, under the nom de plume Bruce Springstone. Chalkley performed a dead-on imitation of Bruce singing the theme song from *The Flintstones*, replete with an intro rap about the quarry workers' "giving their cars a running start with their fat little feet," and "Jungleland"-style moans for Wilma at the end. Almost as good was

Cheech Marin's parody "Born in East L.A." Another milestone of sorts was reached in the same period when Robin Williams started performing as Elmer Fudd singing "Fire." That Williams would choose a song Springsteen had not even released yet can be viewed as a testament to the devotion of those who championed his music through the magic of bootlegging. Springsteen also turned up in a wonderfully funny 1983 Randy Newman song, "My Life Is Good," in which the world's most obnoxious guy imagines Bruce begging, "Rand, I'm tired / Maybe you'd like to be the Boss for a while." And it's not hard to imagine why, during this period, Springsteen proved irresistible fodder for the odd David Letterman routine. ("Pick the subject that is not the subject of a Bruce Springsteen song: (1) Driving down the old highway, (2) Driving with girls, (3) Driving in New Jersey, (4) Sushi.") In 1988 Bruce received the ultimate compliment: a Bob Dylan song on the Traveling Wilburys' first album that made fun of him.

But by the end of 1986, Springsteen himself was feeling worn down, both personally and professionally, and his love-hate relationship with success was beginning to kick into another "hate" phase. Bruce believed that he had "said pretty much all [he] knew how to say about" cars, girls, parents, escape, and hometowns. "I couldn't continue writing about those same things without either becoming a stereotype of myself or by twisting those themes around too much," he recalled. Moreover, given the level of success he had achieved, he did not really feel as if he owned his own work as he once had. He worried about becoming "purely iconic, a kind of Rorschach test that people throw up their impressions upon. . . . You know, you wake up and you're a car commercial." This process was inevitable, he felt. "You put something out there, it gets pulled in and taken up, and becomes part of the culture and part of people's lives. And then you have to reinvent yourself. I felt like that made sense after *Born in the U.S.A.*"

Springsteen was fully aware that any change in direction he now took would not find favor with many of the fans of *Born in the U.S.A.* "Some people will be left behind," he reasoned. "Some new people will come in, and then they'll be left behind. Some people will be there for the duration. You don't have control over that. But the way you keep faith with your audience is by keeping faith with that search."

Springsteen's search mirrored that in a film he often mentioned to interviewers, John Ford's 1956 masterpiece *The Searchers*. In the movie, ex-Confederate soldier Ethan Edwards, played by an aging John Wayne, returns home to find that his family has been massacred and his niece captured by the Comanches. He vows to bring her back and kill the Indians responsible. During his five-year search, he discovers that she has embraced the ways of her captors and so resolves to kill her as well. In the end, following a fierce battle with the tribe, Edwards returns her to "civilization" (her family) but finds that he now feels he has no place there himself. The film ends as he walks off into the horizon alone with his own private demons.

It's hard to believe that Springsteen did not view *The Searchers* as a cautionary tale. "When I was young," he recalled, "I felt excluded from the community and I wanted to gather people around me, to be part of the community. I thought that being a musician, I would succeed. But the opposite happened; the community gathered around me, or rather, around my music, and me, I'm excluded." This feeling helped explain the desperate quality of Springsteen's live performances during the 1970s and much of the 1980s. "I had locked into what was pretty much a hectic obsession, which gave me enormous focus and energy and fire to burn, because it was coming out of pure fear and self-loathing and self-hatred," he later noted. "I'd get onstage, and it was hard for me to stop — that's why my shows were so long." It made for a fantastic evening, but long stretches of unhappiness. Therapy later taught Springsteen that these shows were a form of escape from trying — and failing — to make the human connections he desperately sought.

From early adolescence through his mid-thirties, Springsteen had committed himself to an emotional life focused entirely on music. He had attempted, he realized, to live his life "within the rock 'n' roll dream. It's a seductive choice," he admitted. "The real world, after all, is frightening." In the early days Springsteen could not even find the words to discuss his own inner, or emotional, life. Relationships, he said, were "the hardest thing for me to talk about. I don't know, I'm in the dark as far as all that stuff goes." Back in 1975 Springsteen did allow that while he had lived with one woman for about two years, he refused to consider marriage because "to be married, you had to write married music. And I'm not ready for that."

But now Bruce was more than ready — or at least he thought he was. He and Julianne Phillips, a model and television actress he met in L.A. in the summer of 1984, were wed in May 1985. The Catholic ceremony took place in Phillips's hometown of Lake Oswego, Oregon, with Steve Van Zandt, Clarence Clemons, and Jon Landau standing up as best men. The wedding was conducted in secrecy just after midnight to avoid tabloid publicity, but one of the guests sold his pictures; Bruce said he spied an eight-year-old boy — "a little son of a bitch" — shooting Instamatic photos from the roof during the ceremony.

The new husband told *Newsweek* he was the "happiest" he had ever been. He did not idealize married life but noted that the richness of relationships "lies very often in their struggle, people doing their best, slipping and falling and helping each other back up. And maybe screwing up again, and trying harder." The new record he began work on was designed to illuminate the value of these strivings. Instead, it became a document of Springsteen's efforts to make a failed marriage work.

Bruce knew better than to try to sustain the massive

popularity he enjoyed with *Born in the U.S.A.* He perceived that to try to match its success would both distort his work's content and frustrate his need to expand into new areas. As he explained, he doubted that "the rewards compensate for the single-mindedness, energy, and exposure necessary to meet the demands of the crowd."

Released in the autumn of 1987, *Tunnel of Love* proved an exceptional Bruce Springsteen record in many regards. He had a few extra songs left over this time, but just a few. Springsteen recorded the album alone on guitar, in a makeshift studio over his garage in Rumson, New Jersey, with Roy Bittan playing bass and synthesizer. Other musicians were later added individually and are not featured prominently in the record's mix. Max Weinberg's drums appear lightly on eight cuts. The rest of the band is heard even less frequently; Clarence Clemons's saxophone appears not at all. The recording process took only three weeks, just as *Greetings* had, fifteen years earlier. It was so low-tech that Springsteen's Corvette had to be taken out of the garage to add some piano overdubs. If a passing driver honked his horn at the wrong moment, the entire take would have to be started over again. But according to Springsteen, the album was more meticulously arranged and executed than any of his records since *Born to Run*.

Tunnel of Love returned Springsteen to his natural fan base, with sales of about 3 million copies. Critical reception was typically ecstatic. Tellingly, the album would take all the relevant honors in *Rolling Stone*'s 1987 critics' poll (Best Album, Best Single, Best Songwriter), but none of the top spots in the readers' poll, losing out to U2, REM, and something called Whitesnake.

That so many people who bought *Born in the U.S.A.* passed up *Tunnel of Love* is not surprising. It is an adult album of poetry and meditation that can be called rock 'n' roll only by association. I have to admit that when the record was first released, it left me cold. Being so indifferent to a new Springsteen was a shock to me at the time, but I was twenty-seven and, I suppose, too callow to appreciate its subtlety. Twelve years, one marriage, one divorce, and one child later, I find it Bruce's most moving and perceptive work. It is a beautiful album, an extraordinary journey into the netherworld of intimate conflict — internal conflict, marital conflict, the conflict between faith and flesh, between love and desire, between the desire to love and the ability to do so.

For Bruce, the record "covered an inner life and unresolved feeling that I had carried inside me for a long time." The album's main character, in Springsteen's mind, is the man who was driving the stolen car on "The River," wishing to be caught. He drifts through the night, Bruce explained, as he "confronts the angels and evils that drive him toward his love and keep him from ever reaching" his desire. He embodies, for Springsteen, "the transition my characters made into confronting the more intimate struggles of adult love." Springsteen's characters had become adults who live with the fear that their lives may be passing them by. It is a fear that the desires of their hearts — desires like love, a home, a family, and the ability to find one's place in the world — are now "rushing out the open window of all those cars" they had been driving all night. Springsteen said he cut the record to a rhythm track to provide the music with an aura of a ticking clock, thereby haunting its mood with the incessant passage of time. *Tunnel* speaks to the realizations that Springsteen had made about his own life, in a deeply intimate, though not necessarily literally autobiographical, context. "Knowing that when you make that stand [commitment] the clock starts, and you walk not just at your partner's side, but alongside your own mortal self," he explained, "you name the things beyond your work that will give your life its context and meaning. You promise to be faithful to them. The struggle to uncover who you are and to reach that moment and hold on to it, along with the destructive desire to leave it in ruins," bind together the songs on the album. It is likewise an attempt "to show people striving for that idea of home: people forced out of their homes, people looking for their homes, people trying to build on their homes, people looking for shelter, for comfort, for tenderness, a little bit of kindness somewhere."

Springsteen announces *Tunnel of Love*'s personal/autobiographical nature in the record's opening lines, when he shouts a cappella to a Bo Diddley beat:

I got the fortunes of heaven in diamonds and gold
I got all the bonds, baby, that the bank could hold
I got houses 'cross the country, honey, end to end
And everybody, buddy, wants to be my friend
Well I got all the riches, baby, any man ever knew
But the only thing I ain't got, honey, I ain't got you

The themes of rebellion and escape are not merely absent, but repudiated. Missing, too, are the soaring melodies and fist-in-the-air anthems. The "Mister Bouncer" in "All That Heaven Will Allow" is not a forbidding, repressive figure like virtually all the "misters" of songs past. Almost nothing, in fact, turns out to be as simple and straightforward as it looked from the viewpoint of adolescence. What we get instead are a series of quickly sketched short stories — reminiscent of the works of Raymond Carver in their deceptive simplicity — about people struggling to find themselves a physical, emotional, and spiritual place in the world. The theme of emotional and spiritual — as opposed to physical — searching is what permeates all these stories. "It's easy for two people to lose each other" not out in the world itself, but "in this tunnel of love."

In these complex stories the lessons are hard won, and consequently Bruce is more willing to preach than usual. For example, in an explicit rejection of the romantic view taken in "Born to Run," the road now turns out not to contain the possibility of escape and refuge, but rather offers only false promises and misplaced hopes.

On the road "there's things that'll knock you down you don't even see coming / And send you crawling like a baby back home." The road, Bruce sings, is "nothing but road"; it is at home that one finally finds God's grace.

The album is conspicuous in its use of Catholic imagery. Springsteen's painful religious upbringing had been referred to in his early writing, most particularly in the never recorded "If I Was the Priest," but such references were inevitably irreverent. As he told an interviewer then, "I was raised Catholic, and everybody who was raised Catholic hates religion. They hate it, can't stand it. . . . I quit that stuff when I was in eighth grade. By the time you're older than thirteen, it's too ludicrous to go along with anymore."

By the time he recorded *Tunnel of Love*, Springsteen was no more enamored of orthodox Catholic theological doctrine than he had been as a schoolboy, but the album represents a striking reversal in his attitudes. From the rebellious young delinquent Springsteen has matured into what the sociologist Reverend Andrew Greeley, writing in the journal *America* in early 1988, called a Catholic "liturgist" of singular importance to the contemporary church. Greeley does not concern himself with whether Springsteen agrees with the teachings of the Pope or whether he lives according to Catholic doctrine, questions he regards as "celebrity talk, magazine drivel." For him *Tunnel of Love* has a liturgical dimension because of the artist's repeated efforts to correlate "the self-communication of God in secular life with the

overarching symbol/narratives of his/our tradition."
Greeley also suggests that Springsteen is engaged, intentionally or otherwise, in what he calls a "minstrel ministry," "precisely because his imagination was shaped as
Catholic in the early years of life. He is both a liturgist,
then, and a superb example of why Catholics cannot
leave the church."

Greeley traces Springsteen's piety to "symbol rather
than doctrine." The album is filled with invocations of
light and water, the Easter and baptismal symbols of
the Catholic liturgy. Greeley notes that throughout the
record, prayer, heaven, and God "are invoked naturally
and unself-consciously, as though they are an ordinary
part of the singer's life and vocabulary." In "Two Faces"
the singer gets down on his knees and prays that "love
will make that other man go away." Church bells are
silenced in "One Step Up." In "Cautious Man," the
record's thematic centerpiece, Bill Horton can be found
praying for steadfastness "alone on his knees in the darkness" as the demons of restlessness and lost romance
lead him toward escape. As his wife "lay breathing beside him in a peaceful sleep a thousand miles away," Bill
plots his departure. But finding "nothing but road," he
rushes back to his bedroom, brushes the hair from his
wife's face, and sees the moon shining "on her skin
so white / Filling their room in the beauty of God's
fallen light." This is, Greeley insists, "quite explicitly
a sacrament."

The album is rich with themes of redemption and

grace, but they cannot be won without a struggle. (Billy's tattooed knuckles, with one hand reading "fear" and the other "love," are a powerful symbol of the battle for grace, which Springsteen borrows from Charles Laughton's 1955 film, *Night of the Hunter.*) Spiritual peace must be earned the old-fashioned way — through direct confrontation with the darkness, not at the edge of town but in our own hearts. Bitterness and despair are its promiscuous close cousins.

Is Springsteen aware of just how Catholic his work has become? Greeley says he suspects Bruce "may know what he is doing, but not quite know that he knows." Lest anyone think Springsteen had gone overboard on the religion thing, this impression would have been at least partially dispelled by Springsteen's performance in concert. From the stage, as he drove the audience deeper into delirium, he would assume the demeanor of an old-fashioned fire-and-brimstone preacher and announce to the crowd, "I have sinned. And I don't need no Pat Robertson to forgive me. Pat Robertson can kiss my ass." Moreover, Springsteen was not offering redemption to *everyone.* At a show I attended in Washington, D.C., not long after the outbreak of the Iran-Contra scandal, Oliver North's infamous secretary and fellow document shredder, Fawn Hall, sent word to Springsteen backstage that she and her date, Rob Lowe, would like to come backstage and introduce themselves. Bruce responded with his own note: "I don't like you. I don't like your boss. I don't like what you did. Thank you."

Yet another kind of evidence for the effectiveness with which Springsteen communicates what Greeley terms his "piety" came from the pen of the great Christian existentialist novelist Walker Percy. The writer, who was undergoing radiation treatments at the time, was moved to write Springsteen in 1989: "I've always been an admirer of yours, for your musicianship, and for being one the few sane guys in your field. The two of us are rarities in our professions," he continued, speaking of their shared faith, "you as a postmodern musician and I as a writer, novelist, and philosopher." Percy told Springsteen of his friendship with Flannery O'Connor and of her own complicated relationship with the church. Her faith, Percy intimated, was like Springsteen's — tough-minded but genuine. When facing death and asked whether the symbols of her faith were of any comfort, she replied, "If it's only a symbol, to hell with it." Years later, after Percy's death, Springsteen read his novel *The Moviegoer* and admired its lasting "toughness and beauty." He wrote Percy's widow: "The loss and search for faith and meaning have been at the core of my own work for most of my adult life. I'd like to think that perhaps that is what Dr. Percy heard and was what moved him to write me."

A second striking transformation in Springsteen's writing was the new power and depth he brought to his characterization of women and to all matters of the heart. During the *Born in the U.S.A.* tour, Springsteen sometimes threatened to become a macho cliché, with his muscles bulging and his "hey, little girlie, with your blue jeans so tight" lyrics. Even prior to that, Springsteen's women had not really stood out as distinctive, fully imagined figures. In 1982 the New York chapter of the National Organization of Women even instigated a letter and phone-call appeal directed at him, demanding that he stop referring to women as "little girls" in his songs. NOW's Virginia Cornue complained that Springsteen was "writing and singing sexist music."

In fact, while many of his songs do engage thoughtlessly in prefeminist clichés, they are most often quite sympathetic to their female subjects. Springsteen had never allowed himself any of the typical "my love will save your life" themes upon which so many pop music romances thrive. Even when asking a "little girl" to marry him, he admits, "to say I'll make your dreams come true would be wrong, but maybe, darling, I could help them along." Similarly, when describing his love for the prostitute in "Candy's Room," he demonstrates a degree of empathy that is decidedly novel in the genre. "Strangers from the city . . . bring her toys," he notes, "but no man can keep Candy safe from the sadness all her own."

Still, it is difficult to take a "little girlie" in tight blue jeans seriously or as anything but an invitation to sex. And almost none of Springsteen's songs until then had been written from the point of view of female protagonists. Women were often central to the stories, but they were generally acted upon, rather than actors themselves. This dynamic changes dramatically on *Tunnel of Love*. In "Spare Parts," Janey learns, for instance, as Springsteen announces in the song's video, "the value of her own independent existence" when she decides to sell her engagement ring rather than drown her un-wanted child.

Naturally, Springsteen's conception of manhood changed in conjunction with the shift in his view of women. In "Cautious Man," Bill Horton discovers his soul in remaining true to his family and in reclaiming God's grace in the moonlight on his wife's face. The hero of "Tunnel of Love" learns "to live with what you can't rise above." The protagonist of "Brilliant Disguise" is lost "in the darkness of our love," praying, "God have mercy on the man / Who doubts what he's sure of." In "Walk Like a Man," he prays on his wedding day for the wisdom to profit from his father's example as well as his mistakes. The hardest lesson a man can learn, particu-larly a man who has lived the life of a Springsteen narra-tor, is "when you're alone, you ain't nothin' but alone." What could be more antithetical to the stereotypically romantic notion of American manhood, personified by icons like James Dean, Humphrey Bogart, and Marlon Brando? It's true, Springsteen acknowledges in "Valen-tine's Day," "that he travels fastest who travels alone / But tonight I miss my girl, mister, tonight I miss my home."

Not since Dylan's *Blood on the Tracks* — and perhaps Richard and Linda Thompson's *Shoot Out the Lights* —

had popular music addressed these issues with the degree of emotional complexity one finds in *Tunnel of Love*. Both those records were inspired by impending divorces, and though Springsteen didn't know it at the time, so was *Tunnel of Love*. As Bono would note in his 1999 Hall of Fame induction speech, "A remarkable bunch of tunes, where our leader starts having a go at himself, and the hypocrisy of his own heart, before anyone else could. But the tabloids could never break news on Bruce Springsteen. Because his fans . . . he had already told us everything in the songs. We knew he was spinning. We could feel him free-falling. But it wasn't in chaos or entropy. It was in love."

While Springsteen believed that he was writing and singing about the struggles required to maintain a healthy marriage, in fact he was confronting a relationship that could not be saved. He came to realize he had married the wrong woman. On February 25, 1988, the Tunnel of Love Express opened in Worcester, Massachusetts. As it progressed through the United States and Europe, fans could hardly help noticing that something funny appeared to be taking place onstage. As Clarence Clemons began to fade into the background as Springsteen's dramatic foil, backup singer Patti Scialfa emerged from the shadows, with a winsome, sad-eyed look of devotion on her face. Bruce appeared equally smitten. Springsteen and Phillips eventually separated in April, and the star and his backup singer fell in love.

In Bruce's account, "It went like this: 'Okay fellas. There's gonna be a woman in the band. We need someone to sing all the high parts. How complicated can it get?' Well, a nice paparazzi photo of me in my Jockey shorts on a balcony in Rome . . ." Ms. Phillips filed divorce papers. The media found an irresistible target in Springsteen's failing marriage, in part because he had been so thoroughly canonized until this point. At about the same time, two of Bruce's former roadies, Mike Batlin and Doug Sutphin, sued Springsteen in London. Batlin told reporters that he had resigned from Springsteen's employ after the singer had docked their wages when a canoe at his home was destroyed in a flood.

Although twenty-five-year-old Bruce Springsteen had been traumatized by the onslaught of the celebrity machine when it first feasted on him in 1975, by now he had become pretty well inured to its demands as well as to the pain it was capable of inflicting. He would explain, once the feeding frenzy ended, that he had been preoccupied with the upheavals of his own life, and could not worry about the fact that they were being paraded before the world. "The reality of your own life overwhelms whatever bullshit somebody's written about you in a newspaper for a couple of days," he later explained. Borrowing a concept from Philip Roth, Springsteen said he did not feel a need to respond to this "counterlife that is attached to your own real life by the slimmest of threads. When you reach for and achieve fame," he understood, "one of the byproducts of fame is that you will be trivialized and you will be embarrassed. You will be. I guarantee it. I look at it as part of my job."

Springsteen's divorce from Phillips and his decision to begin a family with Patti Scialfa proved to be just two of the major upheavals in his life as the 1980s ended. He bought a $14 million estate outside of Hollywood, where he and Scialfa decided to encamp for most of the year. In early 1989 he recorded "Viva Las Vegas" for a charity album with a group of L.A. studio musicians, without mentioning the session to anyone else in the band. On September 23 that year the band, including Steve Van Zandt, reconvened at a Jersey Shore club for Bruce's fortieth-birthday party, where they played a magnificently hysterical set for friends and family. But on October 18, 1989, Springsteen made the telephone calls that many observers — though not, apparently, the band members themselves — had long considered inevitable. He individually informed each of his comrades of the past fifteen to twenty years that what the British rock magazine *Mojo* termed "perhaps the greatest backing band in the history of rock 'n' roll" was now itself history. The group had not really been an integral part of Bruce's music for much of the decade. Much of *Born in the U.S.A.* was recorded in 1982. He rejected their contributions to *Nebraska* and used them only sparingly on *Tunnel of Love.* For the live shows on the *Tunnel* tour, Bruce tried to rearrange the band into a new formation for the first time in a decade, but not much changed.

During the parts of the show devoted to the new album and to *Nebraska*, the group was all but anonymous. Springsteen returned them to center stage in 1988 when he toured on behalf of Amnesty International and the fortieth anniversary of the Universal Declaration of Human Rights, but he was already sounding anxious to try new things. "You can get to a place where you start to replay the ritual," he later observed, "and nostalgia creeps in."

Springsteen was eager to rid himself of a decade's worth of expectations, of fans wanting to hear "Born to Run" played the same way every time. "In rock 'n' roll," he told an interviewer as the Amnesty tour commenced, "you work in a very isolated environment. You move from town to town, but you're basically with the same group of thirty people. I wanted to look around." Musically, the Amnesty tour gave Springsteen a chance to branch out a bit, something that clearly appealed to him. He would trade verses with Sting on "The River" and listen to the jazzy riffs of his former bandmate David Sancious, who was playing with Sting and Peter Gabriel. In explaining his painful decision, Springsteen told an interviewer:

The way I look at it is, I get paid to write a new song and I can't keep rewriting the old stuff. I played with a single set of musicians for a long time, and I thought it was time to play with other people. Everybody sings their own spirit, their own personality; it's like a fingerprint, no two musicians play the same or bring to the stage something similar. I think the fundamental values remain. I don't have a plan. I'm just seeing what it is and playing to it. It's going to be a very fun, hard-rocking band. What else it's going to be, I'm just watching it develop.

Each member of the band was paid a significant sum, said to be $2 million, and was also reportedly asked not to give any interviews about Springsteen's personal life. (The *Born in the U.S.A.* tour had earned each member a reported $4 million.) Most took the news as a painful shock, but eventually came to terms with it. Max Weinberg was initially upset not so much with Bruce's wish to explore new musical territory, but "at being left with the legacy that I was fired. . . . That hurt personally and it hurt in the marketplace." He studied for a communications degree and planned to continue in law school before landing his high-profile assignment as the band leader for Conan O'Brien. Roy Bittan bought a studio in Los Angeles, though he was eventually drafted by Bruce for help in his new recording career. Garry Tallent moved to Nashville, where he became a record producer. Danny Federici built a studio in Colt's Neck, New Jersey, where Springsteen has his farm. Nils Lofgren toured with his brother Tom's band. Clarence Clemons, who appeared hardest hit by the news, described his initial feelings as "shocked, hurt, angry all at once." To Clarence, breaking up the band felt like "a divorce." He eventually opened a series of music clubs he named after himself in New Jersey, Florida, and California. Six years later, however, he still spoke in terms of "a big void in music where we used to be." Both Clemons and Lofgren had trouble immediately securing their own major-label contracts.

Springsteen once explained his connection to rock 'n' roll as follows. "To me, the idea is you get a band, write some songs, and go out to people's towns. It's my favorite thing. It's like a circus. You just kind of roll on, walk into somebody's town, and *bang!* It's heart-to-heart. Something can happen to you; something can happen to them. You feel you made a difference in somebody's life." Bruce Springsteen had made a difference to a great many people's lives. Now, he wanted to try to make one in his own.

Well, I took a piss at fortune's sweet kiss

It's like eatin' caviar and dirt

It's a sad funny ending to find yourself pretending

A rich man in a poor man's shirt

— "Better Days," 1992

Caviar and Dirt

Rock stars don't generally have the luxury of suffering wholly private midlife crises, but between 1988, when he ended his last tour with the E Street Band, and 1992, when he finally emerged with two new records and a new band, Bruce Springsteen tried to do just that. Psychologically, Springsteen struggled during much of this period, but not for the usual rock-star reasons. He did not have a problem with substance abuse; he did not believe himself to be trapped by his fame or unworthy of the praise he continually received. Springsteen simply felt lonely and was frightened that that would always be the case. He wanted to address the problem, but he didn't know how.

After the end of the *Tunnel of Love* tour, Bruce and Patti moved to Manhattan briefly, but Springsteen didn't like the city, in part because he couldn't drive around aimlessly. Next he bought a "rich man's house" in the wealthy Republican suburb of Rumson, New Jersey, a town, he noted, where he had been spit on as a teenager when performing with the Castiles.

Living in New Jersey, however, Bruce came to feel "like Santa Claus at the North Pole." Fans would occasionally climb over fences at his house, using the old "Bruce at Graceland" story from 1976 to insist that it was their right. Springsteen worried that he was becoming "a figment of a lot of other people's imaginations" and "enslaved" by his own myth. "It's bad enough having other people seeing you that way, but seeing yourself that way is really bad. It's pathetic. And I got to a place, when Patti and I hooked up, where I said I got to stop writing this story. It doesn't work."

So Bruce and Patti moved to L.A. Springsteen liked the anonymity of the place, which he said left him somehow "just a little lighter, like I was carrying less." He wanted to make a new start. "People always came west to refind themselves or to re-create themselves in some fashion," he later observed. "This is the town of re-creation, mostly in some distorted way, but the raw material is here, it's just what you make it." He also loved the geography of the area. "I like the desert, and a half hour from my house you're in the San Gabriel Mountains, where there's a hundred miles and one store." Believing L.A. to be a place where "a man can really feel his success," as he sang in the clearly autobiographical "Goin' Cali," Springsteen "left his dead skin by the roadside" of a $14 million compound he purchased for his family. This incredible price caused some consternation among fans and in the media. SOME WORKING CLASS HERO! read one headline.

As he settled into his luxurious new life, Springsteen decided that he was paying too high an emotional price for his music. He was great at his job, as he put it, but lousy at the rest of what constitutes a healthy psyche. He was terrified of intimacy. He both desired and feared commitment. He abhorred vulnerability. In other words, he came to understand that he was a great deal better at diagnosing the condition of the human heart in song than he was at dealing with the complications of his own. Crediting Patti's "patience and understanding," he entered therapy and "crashed into myself and saw a lot of myself as I really was." He learned to question his motivations. "Why am I writing what I'm writing? Why am I saying what I'm saying? Do I mean it? Am I bullshitting? Am I just trying to be the most popular guy in town? Do I need to be liked that much?" Eventually, he concluded, "There is no single motivation for anything. You're doing it for all of those reasons."

Having reached a point where he felt he finally knew himself, Bruce decided that it was his fear of failure that paralyzed his ability to commit to relationships. He found that he had "always stopped right before I committed to the place where if it failed, it would really hurt. 'I'm okay up to here but there, no.' It wasn't until I stepped out into that other place that I realized what the stakes were, what the rewards were." After ignoring his emotional state for nearly forty years, he was "taking baby steps," he realized, trying to bring himself "closer to feeling a certain fullness in your life that I always felt like I was missing." Later he could step back and say, "Two of the best days of my life were the day I picked up the guitar and the day I learned how to put it down."

Clearly the biggest change in Springsteen's life was his and Patti's decision to have children. Evan James Springsteen arrived on July 25, 1990.* That night Bruce later recalled:

I got close to a feeling of a real, pure, unconditional love with all the walls down. All of a sudden, what was happening was so immense that it just stomped all the fear away for a little while, and I remember feeling overwhelmed. But I also understood why you're so frightened. When that world of love comes rushing in, a world of fear comes in with it. To open yourself up to one thing, you've got to embrace the other thing as well. And then you embrace those things that you're just around the corner from . . . oh, death, the whole nine yards.

The birth of a grandson also inspired Douglas Springsteen to deepen his relationship with his son in a way that helped make Bruce's own experience of fatherhood "very rich and more resonant." This transformation in

* His sister, Jessica Ray, appeared on December 30, 1991, joined by Sam Ryan Springsteen in January 1994. Bruce and Patti had been married on the lawn of their home on June 8, 1991.

the man who had inspired so much of the fury and frustration that fueled Springsteen's early work was "probably one of the nicest gifts of my life," Bruce allowed.

During the period he was beginning his new family, Bruce Springsteen did not produce a record for nearly five years. For much of this time he did not even try to do so. He was learning, as he said, to put down his guitar, and get a life. When he did pick it up again, he found, "I didn't have a new song to sing. I ended up just rehashing *Tunnel of Love*, and it was all just down and nihilistic." Springsteen tried to break out of his creative funk by inviting Roy Bittan over to work on some of the songs he had written, which would become "Roll of the Dice" and "Real World" on *Human Touch*. But still the old juice just would not flow. He even turned to "little writing exercises" for inspiration, "trying to write something that was soul-oriented or play with existing pop structures." The eventual result was the songs that were included on *Human Touch*, "a lot of which," Bruce has admitted, "is generic, in a certain sense. It was definitely something that I struggled to put together."

The recording began in the spring of 1990. Springsteen and Bittan worked in Bruce's home studio, called Thrill Hill Recording, with Roy on bass and keyboards and Bruce on guitar and vocals. Sometimes they used a drum machine; at others they called in studio musicians. The process was slow and laborious. Unlike previous records, when the problem was winnowing down a wealth of spectacular material, this time they had trouble coming up with an album's worth of decent songs.

Springsteen took several breaks during the drudgery of recording *Human Touch* that resulted in important emotional and artistic breakthroughs. The first was two mid-November 1990 benefit concerts for a Washington public interest organization called the Christic Institute at the Shrine Auditorium in L.A., featuring Bruce, Bonnie Raitt, and Jackson Browne. Both Raitt and Browne were heavily involved in raising money for Central American solidarity organizations and were drawn to Christic, no doubt, because it provided a focus for groups trying to hold current and former officials accountable for crimes committed against Salvadorans and Nicaraguans in the name of anticommunism. Unfortunately, they could hardly have picked a sillier cause than the Christics, who, under the leadership of one Danny Sheehan, were peddling a complicated conspiracy theory regarding U.S. intervention in the region that certainly confused far more people than it enlightened. (The truth was disturbing enough.)

However flawed as a political cause, the concert itself was an artistic triumph. Springsteen had not played a solo acoustic gig since the days he had taken the bus from Asbury Park to Greenwich Village to earn the rent money for his rooms over the old beauty parlor. Clearly nervous as he took the stage, Springsteen asked the audience not to clap along with the songs, for, as he confessed, "It's gonna mix me up."

The songs were a mixture of audacious reinterpretations of old classics, straightforward renditions of songs from *Nebraska*, and new pieces he was still in the process of recording with Roy in the studio. The performances were alternately powerful, chilling, and, on occasion, quite funny. Bruce introduced his ode to cunnilingus, "Red-Headed Woman," dedicating it to both Patti and Bonnie, thanking the latter for the "very, very knowing" kiss she had planted on his lips earlier in the evening.

Even more surprising than his giving his first acoustic performance in two decades was the degree to which Springsteen wanted to open his own troubled psyche to the audience. Sharing such guarded moments is a common feature of people undergoing analysis, but it remains relatively rare to choose an auditorium full of three thousand strangers upon which to unburden oneself. Bruce had been open about his childhood in the past — usually when introducing either an Animals' song or "Growin' Up" — but never before had he elected to reveal his own fears and insecurities to an audience at the same time he was experiencing them.

During the course of his one-hour set, Springsteen spoke at length about the overpowering emotions of fatherhood, of how it felt when, holding his baby son, "I caught his first tear on my finger, seen his first smile, and cleaned up his first shit." He told the crowd of trying to figure out why he felt compelled, when living in New Jersey, to go out at night and continually drive past the house in Freehold where he grew up. His therapist, Bruce reported, suggested to him that "something went wrong, and you keep going back to see if you can fix it or somehow make it right. And I sat there and I said, 'That's what I'm doing.' And he said, 'You can't.'" In introducing "Nebraska," Bruce offered up a similar observation regarding his efforts to heal himself emotionally. "This is a story," he explained, "about disconnection and isolation. It seems hard to stay connected to things. It seems like a lot of work. I've always been fighting between feeling really isolated and looking to make some connection or find some community to belong to. I guess that's why I picked up the guitar."

On the second night of the concerts Bruce decided, perhaps for the first time in his life, to speak publicly about his relationship with his mother. Once again the entry point was his conversations with his therapist. The doctor, Bruce explained, had asked why he wrote so many songs about his father but never any about his mother. "Now, I had to pay for this," he told the crowd good-naturedly, "but you're going to get it for free." He admitted that he found it difficult to sing the next song "because of all the macho posturing that you have to do in rock." Finally Bruce decided that he was "man enough to sing about my mother. I think. I ain't afraid, only a little bit, which is why I'm taking so long. I'm gonna leap into the void of the great line of mother lovers: Richard Nixon, Elvis Presley, Merle Haggard, and every country-and-western singer you ever knew." Springsteen then launched into "The Wish."

> *Last night we all sat around laughing, at the things*
> *that guitar bought us*
> *And I laid awake thinking 'bout the other things*
> *it's brought us*
> *Well, tonight I'm taking requests here in the*
> *kitchen*
> *This one's for you, Ma, let me come right out and*
> *say it*
> *It's overdue, but, baby, if you're looking for a sad*
> *song, well, I ain't gonna play it*

It is a beautiful song and unlike anything else he has ever recorded. Springsteen had not only left it off *Tunnel of Love,* but also chose not to include it on either of the two albums he released in 1992. (It finally appeared on *Tracks* six years later.)

Within a year, Bruce was back in New Jersey for another kind of reunion, this one with Steve Van Zandt, Southside Johnny, Gary Tallent, and Max Weinberg. The occasion was the decision by Van Zandt and Johnny Lyon to reunite and record an album along the lines of the first three wonderfully lush and tough-minded R&B albums that Southside Johnny and the Asbury Jukes recorded in the late 1970s. The band had been signed in the wake of *Born to Run,* but Van Zandt and Lyon had had a falling-out after the third record. Southside

Johnny's career had floundered ever since. Springsteen had written many of his fellow Dr. Zoom member's most popular songs, including his signature song, "The Fever," but had also ended his professional association with the band once Van Zandt did.

For the new album Bruce came into the studio with a partially completed song, "All the Way Home," whose lyrics he continued to revise right up to the moment of recording. (This was a far cry from the days when Van Zandt said he sometimes "just wanted to hit" Springsteen for writing three great songs a night.) The emotional highlight of the record was Van Zandt's composition "It's Been a Long Time," in which all three veterans of the Upstage Club sang nostalgically of sharing the same coat, playing cards until dawn, and sleeping under boardwalks. The group filmed a video at the soon-to-be-shuttered Stone Pony Club in Asbury Park, where the Jukes had been the house band. Bruce never spoke much about the experience, but the rekindled friendship and artistic partnership with his two comrades likely added an important dimension to the reconstruction of his psyche. The reunion was certainly a thrill for fans who felt themselves emotionally invested in the three men's friendship and the sense of community it had once implied.

Creating the new Springsteen record back at Thrill Hill, however, remained an ordeal. Nearly five years after the release of *Tunnel of Love*, Springsteen could barely come up with enough new material to sustain a decent album, much less a typically terrific one. A *Village Voice* writer joked during this period about Springsteen's forthcoming record, *Manitoba*, described as "a tortured masterpiece . . . recorded on a Walkman tape recorder in a broom closet in a small thatched hut on the remote shores of Lake Winnipeg."

Finally, a break came one night when Bruce was driving and listening to Bob Dylan's "Series of Dreams" on the car stereo. Somehow the song inspired him to compose a song describing his feelings on the night of his son's birth. Working by himself in the studio and playing almost all instruments, he came up with an entire album's worth of songs in just eight weeks. Almost all of them are decidedly superior to those he had been struggling with for the previous two years.

Following five solid years of near silence and the breakup of the E Street Band, the simultaneous release of *Human Touch* and *Lucky Town* could not fail to raise fans' expectations. Unfortunately, *Human Touch* turned out to be the weakest record Bruce Springsteen had ever released. Clichés frequently undermine Springsteen's lyrical images, even in the album's best songs. "I Wish I Were Blind" is very nearly ruined by lines like "the message of love that the bluebird brings." In "With Every Wish" Bruce sings of a catfish named Big Jim and yet another bluebird with yet another message of love. "57 Channels (And Nothin' On)," which had been so funny and self-mocking when performed acoustically at the Christic show, became an overblown failed attempt at social commentary. The title song is a worthy continuation of the themes explored on *Tunnel of Love* while it rocks much harder than the songs on that album. But not since "Mary Queen of Arkansas" or "The Angel" had Bruce released such weak material. He offers no specifics about the life crises to which these songs allegedly allude, and settles instead for, as one reviewer put it, "life stinks, and then there's you" songs. Very little on *Human Touch* invites repeated listenings or inspires the kind of interpretive investigations in which fans and critics had so reveled in the past.

Had Bruce not been driving in his car and not been inspired by Dylan to write "Living Proof" and the rest of *Lucky Town*, we might still be reading articles about the death of his creative talent. Given the consistent excellence of *Lucky Town*, Bruce's moment of creative stagnation was over even before the world had the chance to register it.

Since he could not bear to part with *Human Touch*, Springsteen decided to follow the example of the then-supergroup Guns N' Roses and release both records simultaneously, as thematic complements. *Human Touch*, in Bruce's view, is about a man falling from grace, whereas *Lucky Town* deals with his redemption. As he explained, "There's a lot of groping around on *Human Touch* and more on *Lucky Town* about finding your place and refinding yourself, getting back in touch with your own humanity and the good things that you feel about yourself."

Compared with the string of novelistic masterpieces he released between 1972 and 1987, *Lucky Town* is not a great Bruce Springsteen album, but it is at least a powerfully good one, with some of the strongest material Bruce has ever written and recorded. The record's opener, "Better Days," is a thrilling evocation of a man fighting his way out of depression and self-loathing, backed by music as sweeping as that on "Badlands." And "Living Proof" is a miracle of a song: tough, harsh, honest, moving, poetic, and ultimately uplifting all at once. Springsteen describes its subject as the "common strength it takes to constitute a family." Children, he says, "are the 'living proof' of our belief in one another, that love is real. They are faith and hope transformed into flesh and blood." Somehow he manages to capture that feeling and communicate it to people who have never experienced it for themselves.

Well now on a summer night in a dusky room
Come a little piece of the Lord's undying light
Crying like he swallowed the fiery moon
In his mother's arms it was all the beauty I could
  take
Like the missing words to some prayer that I could
  never make
In a world so hard and dirty so fouled and
  confused
Searching for a little bit of God's mercy
I found living proof

I can't say that I decided to change my mind about not wanting children purely on the basis of hearing this song. But the lyrics have haunted me over time, forcing me to reconsider and turn the matter over and over in my mind. Today I sometimes listen to it, holding my own beautiful daughter, and believe it justifies the whole history of rock 'n' roll.

The rest of *Lucky Town* constitutes a pretty fair Bruce Springsteen record, its lyrical content more mature than that on *The River* and its melodies punchier than those on *Tunnel of Love*. "Local Hero" succeeds in self-mockery in a way that "57 Channels" fails to. Springsteen has insisted, moreover, that the story behind its goofy first verse is "completely true. I was driving through a town I grew up in and I looked over and there was a five-and-ten-cent store with a black-velvet painting of Bruce Lee, a picture of me on *Born in the U.S.A.*, and a picture of a dog next to me! I said, 'Wow, I gotta get a photo of that!' It was on sale for $19.99." Springsteen did not have the nerve to buy it himself, however, and sent Patti in after it. "Local Hero" is the happy result. "If I Should Fall Behind" is another one of those perfect country love songs that Springsteen seems able to channel from Hank Willams.

Human Touch and *Lucky Town* entered the U.S. charts at numbers two and three, respectively, and the U.K. charts at one and two. After the initial few days, however, sales fell precipitously. For the first time since *Greetings*, critical reception was mixed. Fans and critics alike were puzzled why Springsteen would end his partnership with the E Street Band only to make records that failed to strike out in any new musical direction. Jon Pareles, writing in the *New York Times*, saw how "the twang of hand-picked guitars and the kick of real drums represent a fortress for a family man, a defense against a postmodern world of rootlessness and moral ambiguity, of synthesized sounds and video games." Writing in the *Village Voice*, however, Tom Carson called Springsteen "a man stuck with a legend that gives him loads of baggage but no destinations, working in a tradition whose compass has shrunk on him, and alternately striving and refusing to endow his ever more insular concerns with continued public resonance as he staves off becoming a million-selling cult artist." Cruelly, Carson concluded, "I'm damned if I don't think he's the new Dylan."

Both discs do share a grizzled, grandfatherly feel when compared with the kinds of records that moved units in the early 1990s. The business was becoming more fragmented than ever. The most popular bands at the time — Nirvana, Guns N' Roses, NWA, Metallica, and Depeche Mode — spoke to a mood of unfocused anger and nihilist depression within extremely narrow musical categories. (You can be certain you would never catch Kurt Cobain or any gangsta rapper singing, "These are better days.") Old-fashioned rock 'n' roll with adult themes about emotional groping and moral and hard-won spiritual redemption accounted for a decidedly small portion of overall sales figures.

The records each sold about 1.5 million copies, roughly half the number of both *Tunnel of Love* and *The River*, and barely a tenth of *Born in the U.S.A.* In England the latter reentered the charts and quickly overtook the two new albums. The numbers spoke for themselves: Bruce Springsteen had become uncool. In Nick Hornby's marvelous rock 'n' roll novel *About a Boy*, in which Kurt Cobain is 1993's superhero, narrator Will Freeman gives himself five "cool" points in a magazine questionnaire for selling all his Bruce Springsteen records. Young people began to regard him as a quaint eighties throwback, not unlike Duran Duran or Martha and the Muffins, only bigger and with more flags.

In interviews, Springsteen feigned indifference about concerns that he had passed his commercial peak. But at the same time, he also took some uncharacteristic steps to help promote the records — steps that were all but certain to alienate some of his most devoted fans. After two decades of refusing to perform on TV, Bruce introduced his new band to the nation on *Saturday Night Live*. He later appeared on MTV's popular *Unplugged*, though he refused to unplug himself. Springsteen also released a live album only in Europe, thereby forcing U.S. fans to pay inflated import prices to obtain it. In what was perhaps his most surprising move, Springsteen played a number of "industry only" shows in small venues, at which fans were barred from purchasing tickets and were not allowed into the room to hear him when a few showed up anyway. (That one of these took place at the Bottom Line, home of the historic 1975 ten-show stand, only made the situation worse.) As Springsteen himself had prophesied in "Lucky Town," fans could no longer "tell his courage from his desperation." Playing "Glory Days" at one of these shows, Springsteen talked not about high school humiliation but about his inability to make a meaningful dent in the sales charts. "I see adventure," he cried. "I see financial reward, I see those albums, man, I see them going back up the charts. I see them rising past that old Def Leppard, past that Kris Kross. I see them all the way up past Weird Al Yankovic even . . . wait a minute, we're slipping. We're slipping down them charts. We're going down, down, out of sight, into the darkness." For longtime devotees, this was truly painful to see and hear. There was a time when the word *darkness* had a deeper meaning to Bruce Springsteen than falling below Weird Al on *Billboard*'s charts.

The celebrity media relished Springsteen's fall from popular grace. *Entertainment Weekly* put him on its cover with the headline WHATEVER HAPPENED TO BRUCE? ("Smells like failure, commercial failure," the story's lead-in began.) The *Village Voice* called him "Rip van Springsteen." While the records may have disappointed, the live shows, however, were still pretty great. At the Meadowlands — where Springsteen complained that his record was now at number "one hundred and fucking five" — eleven nights sold out within two and a half hours. The performances themselves were both terrific and problematic. At forty-two, and despite all his claims of being onstage to hide from real life, he still insisted on playing more than three-and-a-half-hour sets. The band he had assembled showed some flair, though of course its young musicians lacked both the collective spirit and the emotional telepathy that had given his performances with the E Street Band their transcendent quality. But musically, Springsteen found himself for the first time in a quandary. Audiences did not respond favorably to the new material, but what was the point of playing the old warhorses without the band? There was something "sacrilegious," one fan-magazine editor commented, in breaking up the E Street Band just to perform the same old material in the same arrangements but without the boys themselves.

Springsteen did not really know how to address these criticisms. He could not help it if being happy meant he could not write such great rock 'n' roll anymore or play with quite the same degree of nearly insane enthusiasm. He told *Rolling Stone* he felt "Bruced out." Springsteen clearly had no desire to fall into the position of performing as an oldies act, but he began to veer in that direction nevertheless. At the Jersey shows, he even played three songs from *Greetings*, music he had not performed since 1978. After critic Robert Hillburn wrote a tough article in the *Los Angeles Times* arguing that for Bruce to forgo the new material would be a big mistake, however, he resumed performing the songs, assuming that fans would eventually find their way to them.

One aspect of the tour that never received the attention it deserved was how deeply Springsteen had recast his work in the direction of the great soul music that had inspired him ever since he had started playing guitar in Asbury Park. To the degree that *Human Touch* swings at all, it swings as sixties soul, particularly when Bobby King and Sam Moore are on board with backup vocals. Springsteen is rarely given credit for his unselfconscious attitude toward racial integration, an attitude that was reflected in his music as well. Springsteen came of age as an artist, Craig Werner noted, "at a time when white rock was sounding whiter and black music was sounding blacker." Yet the makeup of Springsteen's cover-song repertoire forged the two together. Sam Cooke, Jackie Wilson, Chuck Berry, the Temptations, and Little Richard fused into Elvis, Buddy Holly, Manfred Mann, Mitch Ryder, and Phil Spector, with no distinctions drawn. Moreover, the singer's frequent use of the call-and-response technique was so obviously borrowed from black gospel traditions via sixties soul singers that he eventually turned it into a Baptist preacher parody. And Springsteen unabashedly expropriated some of the time-honored techniques of sixties soul and R&B, from Gary "U.S." Bonds's and Eddie Floyd's roof-raising audience participation numbers to his wonderfully silly James Brown tribute, where the crew would try — and fail — to carry the star off on a stretcher. Like the Godfather of Soul, Bruce would leap off the stretcher, jump on the piano or a nearby speaker bank, and ratchet up the hysteria one more notch.

If Springsteen rarely mentions race in his songs — a race riot appears in "My Hometown" merely as "troubled times" resulting in "fights" and "shotgun blasts" — the character of the band communicated its own powerful message. "We had one of the first integrated bands in rock music — that was something that grew up around Asbury Park," he said once in an interview. "There was racial tension [there], but it was also a place where people mixed." Some critics had a problem with Clarence Clemons's Louis Armstrong–like clowning, and their discomfort was no doubt complicated by the sight of Clarence's hugging and kissing "the Boss" at nearly every performance. Clearly both men viewed this openly expressed physical affection as nothing more than it appeared on the surface: a white kid and a big black guy who genuinely loved each other and got off on the same kind of music.

During the *Born in the U.S.A.* tour, the black nationalist poet Amiri Baraka applauded Springsteen's "ability to translate both the form and content of the blues" and placed him in the pantheon of great "American shouters" alongside James Brown, Wilson Pickett, and Leadbelly. But black people by and large did not much care for Bruce Springsteen or his music. Craig Werner argued that all those fists being thrust in the air struck black audiences as "on the, well, white side." The standing joke was that at a Springsteen concert there were more black people onstage than in the audience. Springsteen himself was bothered by this, for the community of which he spoke so eloquently had never been intended as an exclusively white one. He encouraged the producer Arthur Baker to make "dance" versions of songs from *Born in the U.S.A.*, even giving up artistic control in the process. He participated in Steve Van Zandt's terrific "Sun City" song and video, and traded vocals with Stevie Wonder on "We Are the World." He denounced the KKK from the stage. On the Amnesty tour, Springsteen traveled to Zimbabwe, where at a press conference he explicitly compared the "systematic apartheid of South Africa" to the "economic apartheid of my own country — where we can segregate our underclass in ghettoes of all the major cities." These were radical statements for a mainstream performer to make at the time, and they demonstrated on Springsteen's part a sincere attempt to reach out beyond his typical constituency.

By 1992 Springsteen clearly began trying to shift the locus of his music itself closer to its racially mongrelized Asbury roots. The 1992 touring band was proportionately much more black than white. The music also sounded more soulful than ever before — at least since Steve Van Zandt had left the band. In one miscalculation, Springsteen recast "57 Channels" in a hip-hop vein as a song about the Rodney King riots, with a chant of "no justice, no peace" underlying its now spooky

arrangement. He later told interviewers that he had gone
so far as to record nearly an entire (as yet unreleased) album of hip-hop-inspired songs, though he was clearly a
great deal more comfortable with the soul music of his
past than the styles of the present. If Springsteen never
ultimately managed to achieve the racial crossover status he sought, he did succeed in reclaiming his own soul
roots. Bruce Springsteen was playing "black music" in a
historically significant sense. But black people themselves didn't really listen to that kind of music any longer.

At the end of the tour Springsteen returned home to
L.A. and seemed to vacillate between embracing the
celebrity culture that surrounded him and seeking to fall
back into the habits and habitats in which he had felt so
comfortable as a young musician. One night he played at
a private Hollywood party with a nightmarish band
that included Woody Harrelson, Dan Aykroyd, Wesley
Snipes, and Magic Johnson. Only a few weeks later he
performed for about a hundred people with John Wesley
Harding at McCabe's Guitar Shop in Santa Monica. He
also joined the house band at the L.A. House of Blues
for a rendition of a bunch of obscure old blues songs.
Toward the end of the year, he popped up with Jackson Browne at the Love Ride XI, a big motorcycle rally
outside L.A., where the two of them played "Born to
Run." Bruce had had to tape the lyrics to the back of his
guitar because he could no longer remember them,
though he apparently did much better with the biker anthem "Born to Be Wild."

Perhaps the most surprising of these impromptu gigs was one at the American Booksellers' Association's annual convention when Bruce took the stage with a pickup band of writers called the Rock Bottom Remainders. There, in the company of Dave Marsh, Stephen King, Dave Barry, Amy Tan, and Matt Groening, Bruce was introduced as "a guy who isn't up to our musical standards, but we'll let him play anyhow." In Barry's inimitable rendering, the event took place during an unexpected demand from the booksellers for an encore:

So we went back on stage, and I picked up one of the two guitars I'd been using, and just as we were about to start, Stephen tapped me on the shoulder and said, "We have a special guest." I turned around, and there was Bruce Springsteen. I still don't know how he came to be at this convention; I don't believe he's a bookseller. All I know is, he was picking up the other guitar. My guitar.

"Bruce," I said to him. "Do you know the guitar part to 'Gloria'?" This is like asking James Michener if he knows how to write his name. "I think so," he said. So we played "Gloria," and I say in all modesty that it was the best version of that song ever played in the history of the world, going back thousands of years. I would shout, "G–L–O–R–I-I-I-I-A"; and the band, including Bruce Springsteen, would respond, "GLORIA!" and the crowd would scream as only truly receptive booksellers can scream. I could have died happy right then.

In a more serious musical vein, Springsteen spent much of the year helping to produce Patti Scialfa's solo record, *Rumble Doll.* He also teamed up with Jonathan Demme to write the theme song to his forthcoming movie,

Philadelphia, in which Tom Hanks plays a gay lawyer with AIDS suffering from the kind of discrimination that routinely accompanied the illness when it first appeared.

Released in April 1994, the film played a powerful role in raising consciousness about the problems that even the most privileged members of society encounter when faced with the debilitating disease. Springsteen's song "Streets of Philadelphia" proved no less influential. The song is a poetic journey into the fear and loneliness that accompanies the isolation of AIDS. It proved to be the first hit single ever sung by a heterosexual man in the voice of a homosexual one, a voice that draws added power from Springsteen's former image as a macho man, now traveling "a thousand miles, just to slip this skin."

Springsteen originally recorded a jazzier version of the song, which included Ornette Coleman on trumpet and Little Jimmy Scott on background vocals, but characteristically he decided that he preferred the original demo. Scott had been filmed for the video, and a press release was issued announcing as much, but he was cut out of that as well. In its final version Bruce appeared alone, walking down the city's streets, singing yet another version of the song, since he now refused to lip-synch his videos, having been so unhappy with his experience in "Dancing in the Dark."

"Streets of Philadelphia" successfully rejuvenated Springsteen's reputation, both critically and commercially. As Ann Powers noted, Springsteen succeeded in crossing "the barriers of class, race, and gender. We all have different ideas of the good life. But when we hurt, 'Philadelphia' suggested, 'we become equals in our solitude and our terrible wish for communion.'" Politically, the song positioned Springsteen exactly where he wanted to be: out in front on an issue to which the only opposition came from ignorance and intolerance. (He later made donations to the South Philadelphia playground featured in the video, to the AIDS organization amfAR to help pay for the premiere of the film, and to the AIDS Project LA, where he sang the song live for the first time.) To no one's surprise, in 1995 "Streets of Philadelphia" swept the Oscars and the Grammys, and Springsteen performed it at both ceremonies.

In yet another atypical action, Springsteen built upon the award show publicity with a quickly packaged greatest hits album. Columbia had wanted one for nearly two decades, but Springsteen had rejected the idea as too grossly commercial. Before finally agreeing to the concept, he decided to call the members of the E Street Band — including Steve Van Zandt — and asked them to show up in New York within seventy-two hours to record a few more songs. It would be the first time the band was in a studio together since the days before *Born in the U.S.A.*, more than a decade earlier. (Nils Lofgren had never recorded with the group.) The release deadline ensured that the studio time would be as intense as ever, with twenty-hour workdays built into the schedule.

While the record he released on February 28, 1995, was labeled *Bruce Springsteen's Greatest Hits,* it had little in common with any greatest hits package save one or two by Bob Dylan. Of Springsteen's twelve top-ten singles, only seven were included on the disc. "I'm on Fire" and "Cover Me" were both bigger "hits" than the single of "Born in the U.S.A.," but the latter appears on the record and the former two do not. The compilation opens with "Thunder Road," even though it was never released as a single. (Nothing at all from *Greetings* or *Wild & Innocent* made the cut.)

Finally, the record featured four songs that he had never released before, which ensured that die-hard fans would buy the record, even though they already owned three-quarters of the music on it. This tactic rightly angered some, as Springsteen could just as easily have put them on a low-cost EP instead. Once again, it appeared that it was longtime supporters who were paying the cost for Springsteen's desire to maximize his popularity. Nevertheless, fan purchases, plus all the publicity accompanying the Grammy awards, helped the record enter the U.S. and U.K. charts at number one.

The new songs were, as usual, uneven in quality. In the video of the recording sessions that Springsteen later released, entitled "Blood Brothers," Landau seems to promise the inclusion of "Frankie," one of the lost classics that turned up only on inferior-quality bootlegs. The band also completes two takes of a soaring love song called "Back in Your Arms Again" with a wonderfully passionate Springsteen vocal, but it fails to appear even on the special *Blood Brothers* EP included with the video.* Instead, *Greatest Hits* offers "Secret Garden," which was intended for another *Tunnel of Love*–type album that Springsteen said he recorded in 1994. This rather plodding ode to the mysteries of love and sex — containing Bruce's first explicit blowjob reference — became Springsteen's eighteenth Top 40 hit single when it was chosen for a key romantic moment in the smash Tom Cruise movie *Jerry Maguire.*

"This Hard Land," however, was a classic outtake from *Born in the U.S.A.* and would have proved superior to much of what did make it onto the album, though the gender confusion it evinces in its lyrics might have subverted the macho image Springsteen was then cultivating. "Murder Incorporated," a powerful locomotive of a song, had also been planned for *Born in the U.S.A.* Bruce later explained that he selected it as a favor to an anonymous fan. "For years," he explained, "there's this guy that's been following me around with a 'Murder Incorporated' sign. I see him in the audience, like, every five shows. I have never played the song, ever, in concert, and would have no intent to do so, and yet this guy follows me around with this sign and flashes it during the entire show. So it was he who I had in mind when we put the

* It finally made it onto *Tracks* in 1998.

song on the album. We said, 'Let's put this on for that guy, whoever he is.'"

The final new song on the record, "Blood Brothers," was written just before Springsteen began recording with his old comrades, when he had been visited by "the ambivalence and deep affection of revisiting a relationship spanning twenty-five years." The ambivalence might have been related to the implicit admission that Springsteen could have handled the matter of the dissolution of the E Street Band with greater sensitivity, plus the fact that he had not really succeeded in finding the musical direction he had been seeking. In any case, it contains some strangely melancholy lyrics, for a man writing about the joys of reunion.

> *Now I don't know how I feel, I don't know how I*
>   *feel tonight*
> *If I've fallen 'neath the wheel, if I've lost or I've*
>   *gained sight*
> *I don't even know why, I don't know why I made*
>   *this call*
> *Or if any of this matters anymore after all*

Springsteen later remarked, "I guess I wrote it the night before I went in the studio with the band, and I was trying to sort out what I was doing and what those relationships meant to me now and what they mean to you as you move through your life. Basically, I guess I always felt that the friendships, the loyalties, and the relationships, those are the bonds that keep you from slipping into the abyss of self-destructiveness. And without those things, that abyss feels a lot closer."

Whether Springsteen was, at this point, slipping further toward or away from that abyss was something only he could know as he climbed back to number one, on the achievements of his past.

The highway is alive tonight . . .

— "The Ghost of Tom Joad," 1995

The Ghosts of Bruce Springsteen

From a fan's standpoint at least, the deeply antici-
pated reunion of the E Street Band turned out to
be a disappointment. The group did a couple of
"friends and industry only" gigs for video shoots
and publicity purposes, but Springsteen refused
to schedule any public concerts or consider a new
tour. The only opportunity for fans to see the band was a
disastrous spot at a Labor Day 1995 stadium concert to
celebrate the opening of the Rock and Roll Hall of Fame
in Cleveland. The band played a leaden "Shake, Rattle
and Roll" and passing versions of "She's the One" and
"Darkness on the Edge of Town" and then backed up
both Jerry Lee Lewis and Chuck Berry. In the latter case,
Berry did what he had always done — ignored the musicians with whom he was playing. The band ended up re-
peating its unhappy experience of trying to back him up
in a club twenty-two years earlier. Springsteen left the

stage looking angry and annoyed. (He later sang an acoustic "Forever Young" with Dylan, but this proved far more memorable for the emotional resonance of the image — like old photos of Babe Ruth and Lou Gehrig — than for either artist's musical performance.)

Instead of touring with his own band that year, Springsteen decided to accept a nonpaying gig as a guitarist in the band of rocker Joe Grushecky. The singer/guitarist was uncannily reminiscent of Springsteen and had had a career that resembled a Dickensian *Christmas Carol* version of what Bruce's might have been if *Born to Run* had never happened. Grushecky's songs, drawn from the gritty working-class lives of Pittsburgh steelworkers, focused on downbeat domestic dramas shadowed by economic hard times. The two men even sported identical goatees, with equivalent ratios of brown to gray. With his band, the Iron City House-rockers, Grushecky had released four excellent albums on MCA between 1979 and 1983 but since then had lost his major-label support and could no longer support his family through his music. Despite his having had what Greil Marcus called "the best hard rock band in the country" in 1980, his orthodox approach to rock music had failed to inspire commercial success.

Grushecky had had an earlier album coproduced by Steve Van Zandt but was now feeling a bit desperate. He swallowed his pride and contacted Landau, asking for Bruce's help. Springsteen decided to undertake for

Grushecky a modified version of what he and Van Zandt had done for Gary "U.S." Bonds and Southside Johnny. He cowrote one song, produced and played on a new record, and found him a company to release it. The result, titled *American Babylon*, is good clean rock 'n' roll. Its socially conscious lyrics combined with stinging guitar solos constitute an impressive, though unspectacular, return to the hard-nosed music of the late seventies and early eighties.

Before the record or tour was announced, I received a tip, while on vacation, that Springsteen would be joining Grushecky at a gig scheduled at a Jersey Shore bar called Tradewinds. I called up the club and was told that Bruce *had* practiced with the band the night before. I ordered a ticket for all of ten dollars — including the service charge — and borrowed a car and drove from the tip of Long Island to the Jersey Shore, trying not to get my hopes up too much. I remembered all the plane, train, and automobile trips I had taken in years past because some bar had announced a show by a performer who was said to be a friend of Bruce's, or had recorded one of the songs he gave away, or had been an oldies act whose career he had revived, or who sounded a lot like Bruce (who was said to approve), or had been in the E Street Band once, and the two were said to still be in close contact. I had seen some wonderful shows by Southside Johnny, Beaver Brown, Gary "U.S." Bonds, Steve Earle, Steve Van Zandt's Disciples of Soul, and Clarence

Clemons's Red Bank Rockers, but almost all of them had been marred by drunken louts shouting, "Brooooce!" between every song. Not only was it cruel to the performers, it made the rest of us feel like even bigger fools for continuing to hope that he might show.

Grushecky and his band came on about midnight with no sign of Bruce. I began getting that familiar sinking feeling in my stomach, now magnified by my advancing age. Then I noticed Tim Robbins and Susan Sarandon bopping to the recorded music in a corner near the stage. Immediately, I felt a little worse but a lot better. Worse, because Bruce really should not be hanging around with movie stars, even talented, lefty ones, but better because HE WAS HERE. After twenty years of trying, I was finally going to see Bruce Springsteen in a bar! On the Jersey Shore! And, there was Steve Van Zandt right next to him, just the way he should be. They were singing "Lucky Town," which would not even place among the songs I would have chosen, but no one was complaining. Max Weinberg showed up a little while later to play drums. For the next two hours, they alternated between Bruce's songs, songs from *American Babylon*, and great old stuff like "Gloria," "Mustang Sally," "Diddy Wah Diddy," and "Down the Road Apiece." They closed with the "Ramrod" to end all "Ramrod"s. The police even lifted the local curfew in celebration of this blessed event. The big, stupid football player behind me kept yelling, "Thunder Road," and spilling beer on my back, but what could I do but forgive him? These were better days.

The person to whom I owed my good fortune that night was someone I have never met and whose name I still do not know. He passed on the information in a private e-mail, during the course of a conversation inspired by my own obtuseness. I had only recently ventured into cyberspace, and in discovering America Online's Springsteen bulletin board, I found myself thinking that the people who frequented it were maybe a little crazy. Somebody named Hal was talking about flying from L.A. to New York to see Bruce sing a single song at a celebrity rain forest benefit. (Hal knew more about Bruce than Bruce himself did, and he wanted you to know it.) Others were arguing about angels-on-the-head-of-a-pin-type arcana relating to the hidden meanings of various songs; the relative merits of Bruce's hired drummer, Zachary Alford, on the 1992 tour; and whether, at any one point during the previous twenty-three years, Bruce had ever performed a note of "The Angel" in public. Later, on the Springsteen mailing list "LuckyTown Digest," I came across an argument as to whether Bruce played his greatest version of "Backstreets" on March 4, 1977, in Jacksonville; March 25, 1977, in Boston; December 15, 1978, in San Francisco; or December 31, 1978, in Cleveland. The various participants had bought multiple versions of bootlegs they already owned because of better microphone placement by the person standing in the audience, holding the little tape recorder.

I apparently let slip my amazement at what I had discovered and soon received an e-mail asking just what was so terrible about a group of people who shared a passion that I evidently held myself but who shared it more passionately? I had to admit the sender had a point. We e-mailed a few more times, and eventually he was good enough to pass along the Jersey bar tip to me. My unknown correspondent has my eternal gratitude.

According to the Oxford English Dictionary, the word *fan* probably derives from the England of the 1600s, where it was most often used as an abbreviation for *fanatic*. Fanatics were usually religious zealots considered by their neighbors to be mad, or perhaps possessed. This definition would handily apply to a few Springsteen fans, particularly those who hang around backstage at the end of every show, hoping for a nod or a wink or, even better, an opportunity to touch the hem of their hero's garment. (It is such behavior that necessitates the presence of Springsteen's longtime bodyguard, Vietnam special forces veteran Terry Magovern.) For some of these people, worship of Springsteen is really no different from that attending any other celebrity, from the bobbysoxers who screamed themselves silly at the Paramount Theater for Frank Sinatra to the older female fans in Las Vegas who faint at the prospect of being handed a sweat-soaked handkerchief by Wayne Newton.

But my own experience of Springsteen fandom is that precious little of it fits these traditional contours. Most fans enter the world of Springsteen with the same respect, devotion, and serious-mindedness that religious individuals enter a church. (More than one commentator has remarked on seeing Springsteen fans "standing on their chairs, extending their arms the way fundamentalist worshipers do during church services.") The music is the canon, the concerts are the ceremony, but Bruce is not, after all, the savior. For if Springsteen's music communicates any one message, it is that redemption can only come from within and must be earned. The overall experience of the music helps fans order their worlds, draw strength for their tribulations, and share, with a community of like-minded individuals, their moments of extreme emotion — be it happiness or pain. In preparing to write this book, I asked a few members of various online discussion groups to answer the question, as succinctly as possible, Why does Bruce matter? Here are the first five answers I received:

- "He makes me feel like I belong in this world."
- "Bruce Springsteen's art keeps my conscience alive."
- "He matters to me because he is like my backup heartbeat."
- "His music creates an internal dialogue that [helps] us discover who we are."

- "He has opened places in my mind, provided me with music to live my life, given me solace in my grief, provided me with joy for celebrations, introduced me to lifelong friends, raised my blood pressure, increased my heart rate, added smile lines to my face, and made me dance on a folding chair and scream, 'Gooba, gooba, gooba.'"

These comments were by and large made by adults with families, commitments, and relatively normal lives. The discovery of the invisible church of Springsteen fandom has provided them with a means to face perhaps the most important spiritual void in postmodern American life: our lack of an authentic language of the heart and of a genuine community with whom it can be shared. No wonder so many fans speak of their first exposure to Springsteen as a kind of supernatural event.

Springsteen fandom takes on many forms, almost all of them involving what most people would consider extraordinary, even ridiculous degrees of effort to attend a typical rock concert. Some Springsteen fans organize themselves into communal ticket-buying agencies, so that no one is forced to pay scalpers' fees to get inside the doors of a concert hall. One of my correspondents told me of how he and a group of fans who met online pooled their money, chartered a bus, and then worked the phones together, finally traveling to Wallingford, Connecticut, to see Springsteen there. Almost the entire bus ended up with tickets in the first twelve rows. Another person wrote me of a wedding reception he attended one morning in Chicago. The Springsteen fans among them — including the bride and groom — left the party and drove straight through in their gowns and tuxedos to Urbana, where they had seats in the balcony of the arena. As the newlyweds approached the venue, two anonymous fans noticed what was up and exchanged their fifteenth-row tickets as a wedding present. The couple named their first child Terry, after the heroine of "Backstreets."

My own nomination for the Springsteen fan MVP award is a woman named Mary-Ellen Breton. Beginning two years ago, Mary-Ellen organized an ongoing annual online auction of Springsteenania — bootlegs, old magazine cover stories, rare records and photographs — to raise money for the Kristen Ann Carr Fund of Memorial Sloan-Kettering Cancer Center. (Ms. Carr died in January 1993 of liposarcoma. She was the daughter of Barbara Carr, who works for Springsteen via Jon Landau Management, and stepdaughter of Springsteen biographer Dave Marsh.) The fund, begun with $1.5 million raised at a 1993 Springsteen concert at Madison Square Garden, pays for both sarcoma research and support services for young adults, teenagers, and other sarcoma patients. So far, Mary-Ellen's heroic solo effort has raised $10,000 for the KACF, in addition to another $4,600 for World Hunger Year. (The online address for future KACF auctions is www.brucelegs.com.)

Springsteen has said, "I always wanted my music to

influence the life you were living emotionally, with your family, your lover, your wife, and at a certain point, your children." Daniel Cavicchi, who has devoted an entire book to the study of Springsteen fans, has noted that many go through Springsteen's records as if they were looking at a personal photo album, marking the events of their lives in relation to dates of record releases and concerts.

Springsteen's relationship with his fans is, from a moral standpoint, his most sacred trust. Without their sustained devotion over the past decades, it might well have been he who would be calling up rock stars and asking their help to find a respectable record label to give voice to his art. But the relationship is complicated by the contemporary collapse of all boundaries between celebrities, fans, and the celebrity-mad mass media, to say nothing of the thankfully rare phenomenon of the stalker. Springsteen has been quite fortunate in the degree of freedom with which he has been able to lead his life. He can still take his family bowling in New Jersey or go out to dinner in Manhattan without too much fear of harassment. He is happy to say hello, though autographs appear to depend on his mood. The extraordinary actions he occasionally undertakes for an individual fan, however, suggest his attitude to the fan base as a whole, particularly since they are impossible to stage and are often decided upon with remarkable casualness. Sometimes they involve no more than his picking up a hitchhiker on a New Jersey highway. Most famous is the dinner-with-the-family story in St. Louis after *Stardust Memories*. In early 1999 nineteen-year-old Middlebury College sophomore and international-relations major Adam Schlidge invited Bruce to be his guest on his 100-watt college radio show. They had met two years earlier, in a Jersey gym, where both worked out with the weights. Springsteen did the show for a full hour. On a more exalted, if slightly less quirky scale, one woman wrote me of a story involving a part-time volunteer with the Make-A-Wish Foundation in Miami. A terminally ill boy had requested an autographed copy of *Born to Run*. After repeatedly receiving no response from Springsteen's people for several weeks, she suddenly received a call one afternoon asking if the boy would be home the following day. The volunteer interpreted this to mean they would be sending something special via courier. Instead, Springsteen himself showed up with the album and proceeded to spend the afternoon with the dying boy. He insisted that no media be informed of the visit, and I have never seen any account of it elsewhere.

"You imagine of Springsteen," Eric King once wrote, "that he is the first rock star who dreams of being his audience as much as his audience dreams of being him." What is most significant about the relationship between Springsteen and his fans is not his extraordinary gestures toward them or the imputed dreams each has, but the consistent sense of mutual respect and regard that exists between them. Springsteen recognizes his responsibility in this regard and indeed, defined it for himself at the beginning of his career. "I very consciously set out to develop an audience that was about more than buying records," he said. "I set out to find an audience that would be a reflection of some imagined community that I had in my head, that lived according to the values in my music and shared a similar set of ideals." The fans, in turn, have always expected Springsteen to keep faith with those ideals. Asked about this in 1996, Springsteen responded:

When I separated from the E Street Band, there was tremendous feedback from the fans. Some fans were hurt because I think one of the values of my music was about loyalty, friendship, and remembering the past. So at some point, the question becomes, How do you stay true to those values but yet grow up and become your own man? And I think I've tried to thread my way through those things as best as possible. And I think I've done pretty good. I certainly haven't done perfectly, and of course, it ain't over yet. But I think that basically you know there's a certain amount of things that every fan creates for you in their head that may not be completely you in any fashion. I think the pressure to be grounded and for fans to feel like you're speaking to them in some fashion is good. That's what I want to do. But you also want to make the music you want to make, live the life that wherever the road you're traveling on leads you, and live with the contradictions that are a part of finding the large audience and having the success in the world that you live in.

It is Bruce's willingness to try to live up to these words that gives his relationship with his fans its special quality. And it is his occasional transgressions against them, rather than anything having to do with his private life, that have proved most painful to the members of his invisible church.

Lest any confusion remain on this point, Bruce Springsteen is no saint. Were one to list the counts of a moral indictment one by one, they would look something like the following: Springsteen may well have mistreated the then loyal employees who sued him after they were fired. He allowed himself to be talked into a few commercial compromises he probably should not have made, particularly during the *Born in the U.S.A.* period and when his two albums failed to sell in 1992. (In fact, most writers tend to paint Landau as the heavy in those decisions.) He makes far too much of charity donations that constitute a minuscule fraction of his fantastic wealth. And he sometimes behaves a bit disingenuously, pretending not to care about the privileges and associations that his wealth and celebrity bring him, while indulging them on other occasions.

Springsteen himself makes it difficult to know just how much truth lies in these charges. He is fiercely — and wholly understandably — protective of his privacy. Upon pain of firing, his employees are forbidden to give interviews about him. Dave Marsh noted that "only people as concerned with control as Bruce himself could have worked with him successfully, and the first principle of control is to keep the spread of information within the tightest limits possible. Once information is widely shared, particularly once the public has access to it, control seeps away." Springsteen's pose of affected insouciance regarding his public image is therefore at odds with the considerable effort that goes into controlling it. (Unfriendly critics have called Springsteen the first rock star to have his own ministry of propaganda.)

But how can one reasonably judge the life decisions of a man faced with the choices that megastardom demands? Compared with the way other contemporary rock stars of similar stature have behaved, Springsteen need make few apologies. Any examination of the private lives of Elvis Presley, Bob Dylan, John Lennon, Mick Jagger, Keith Richards, David Bowie, Michael Jackson, the members of Led Zeppelin, the Who, the Grateful Dead, Frank Sinatra and the entire Rat Pack, or just about any other comparably successful pop culture idol would be to Springsteen's advantage.

"Show me a hero, and I'll write you a tragedy," quipped that other great romantic Catholic American poet of modern disenchantment, F. Scott Fitzgerald. Whatever validity that assessment may have, it is fundamentally misguided when we apply it to artists with a public stature. As difficult as it may be to remember in our celebrity-obsessed culture, it is not the artist we grow to respect and trust, but the art itself. Whether Mozart or Miles Davis was cruel to the members of his family is an issue apart from and irrelevant to the genius of each one's art and can hardly be said to interfere with our appreciation of it today. As Springsteen himself observed, "Somebody can do real good work and be a fool in a variety of ways. I think my music is probably better than I am. I mean, like, your music is your ideals a lot of times, and you don't live up to those ideals all the time. You try, but you fall short and disappoint yourself."

Assuming the public image of Bruce Springsteen is not a complete and colossal fraud — which would itself be a considerable accomplishment in today's Peeping Tom celebrity culture — his significance to the world beyond his immediate circle of acquaintances lies entirely in the impact of his art. Springsteen assesses his relationship to his audience as follows: "The idea is that you and your audience learn together, you ferret out your illusions. That's what my work is about — people stumbling across their illusions, letting them drop by the wayside, then trying to find something that's real." "Real" or not, Springsteen's media personality is ultimately irrelevant to his success in achieving the goals he describes. There is simply no faking the feeling he both demonstrates and inspires through the wondrous force of his performance. And if he were somehow "faking it," what would it matter? The result would be the same either way.

The second half of the 1990s found Bruce Springsteen reconnecting powerfully to those aspects of his art that earned him so many devoted fans during the previous two decades: his willingness to forgo commercial concerns to address what was most deeply disturbing about the society in which he lived and his love for and loyalty to the people who had helped him make his music.

After his brief bar tour with Grushecky, Springsteen released his second solo album of Guthriesque hurt songs, this one even sadder and darker than *Nebraska*. On a few of the songs on *The Ghost of Tom Joad*, Springsteen barely even bothers with melodies, so intent is he on focusing attention on the harsh world inhabited by his characters, almost all of whom live on the physical and psychic margins of American society. As music, *Tom Joad* was only intermittently successful. Its songs tend to run into one another, and its sparse production requires the listener's full attention at all times. Putting the disk on the CD player can feel like a moral obligation. But its rewards are substantial.

Although it had expressed itself only sparingly in his recordings during the previous decade, Springsteen's political conscience had continued to develop in the wake of *Nebraska* and *Born in the U.S.A.* The Tunnel of Love Express may have been apolitical, but it culminated in one of the most politically meaningful moments of Springsteen's life. On July 19, 1988, about eighteen months before the Wall came down, Springsteen played one of the largest and most dramatic rock concerts in all of history, in East Berlin, capital of what was then the German Democratic Republic (GDR). With approximately 160,000 people present, the stadium held an audience equivalent to 1 percent of the country's entire population. The official GDR press release noted that "Springsteen, born in 1949 into a working-class family, in many of his songs attacked social misery and injustice in his native country." When Springsteen introduced Dylan's "Chimes of Freedom," he told the audience, "I want to tell you, I'm not here for or against any government. I came to play rock 'n' roll for you East Berliners — in the hope that one day all the barriers will be torn down. I thank you." The concert was broadcast on both state television and radio on a time delay, and this statement of Springsteen's was censored. A few months after returning to the United States, he released "Chimes of Freedom" on an EP to raise money for Amnesty International before embarking on yet another world tour to promote the fortieth anniversary of the International Declaration of Human Rights.

It may have been the uniformly positive reaction to "Streets of Philadelphia" that inspired Springsteen to try to return his political interventions to a more human musical scale. That record, Springsteen allowed, sent him "down a particular road," as he explained to one concert audience. But he had long been inspired by the example of Woody Guthrie, as well. In addition to the Guthriesque *Nebraska*, Springsteen had been eager to be a part of 1988's *Vision Shared* tribute album, recorded to raise money for the Smithsonian Institution to save Moses Asch's Folkways Records following his death. He contributed to the record spirited versions of Guthrie's "Vigilante Man" and "I Ain't Got No Home."

Tom Joad is perhaps Bruce Springsteen's most uncompromising album. It demands that we meditate, however briefly, on the lives of people most of us attempt to keep out of sight: male hustlers, homeless people sleeping on grates, Mexican migrants cooking methamphetamine in the California desert. These characters are the lost souls of *Nebraska* a decade later, with what remained of their hopes destroyed and their future behind them. The songs raise uncomfortable questions about the illusions we share and the lies we embrace in order to get through the day believing in our fundamental decency. It is written and sung, in other words, in the tradition of moral prophecy.

There is, to be sure, no direct equation between prophecy and good music. Some of Bob Dylan's greatest triumphs as well as his most embarrassing mistakes fall into this same category. Springsteen's work in this genre is on a more even keel. Like Guthrie before him, he was initially inspired by John Ford's film of John Steinbeck's novel *The Grapes of Wrath* to tell Tom Joad's story in song. The link is notably direct, though the characters have been updated, and their races and genders expanded to account for life along the U.S.-Mexican border. Also like Guthrie, Springsteen inserts actual dialogue from the Ford film into his lyrics. The songs are, if anything, even more profoundly painful than Guthrie's, as if Springsteen were attempting to unite Guthrie's social concern with the almost supernaturally dark cadences of

Robert Johnson, in a voice as sad and weary as Hank Williams's at the end of his rope.

For *Tom Joad* to have been fully successful, Springsteen would have had to accomplish all of the above and more. The romantic notion of "the people" had undergone considerable transformation since Tom's mother invoked its invincibility at the end of Ford's 1932 saga. By the end of the century "the people" had become a confusing amalgam of races, genders, and sexualities who demonstrated precious little proclivity to think of themselves in collective terms. Springsteen's rhetoric from the stage sometimes sounded as if he thought he might be able to wish this problem away. In song, however, his art was truer to the depressing reality of cultural and psychological isolation surrounding the lives of his characters.

Springsteen explained that the musical aspects of *Tom Joad* are intentionally minimal. "The simplicity and plainness, the austere rhythms defined who these characters were and how they expressed themselves." His hope was to disappear almost entirely into his characters. "When you get the music and lyrics right in these songs, your voice disappears into the voices of those you've chosen to write about," he noted. "To get to the emotional center . . . you pull out of yourself . . . the commonality you feel with the man or woman you're writing about." While the chosen subject matter has an inescapably preachy feel to it, there is little of the typical protest-song instruction-manual mentality that characterizes so much sixties-style folk music. "You can't tell people what to think. You can show them something by saying, 'Put these shoes on, walk in these shoes.'"

The "shoes" on *Tom Joad* are torn and tattered. They have been passed along through poor immigrant families by fathers without work and mothers without hope. In many cases the songs were inspired by actual events. Springsteen would on occasion read a story in the newspaper and track down its reporter to get as many of the details as possible. He wrote "Youngstown" and "The New Timer," for instance, after reading a book called *Journey to Nowhere: The Saga of the New Underclass* by Dale Maharidge and Michael Williamson. The authors had traveled the country for three months in search of the stories of modern-day transients, forced by economic circumstances to abandon their homes and try to survive on the road. Springsteen said he had been moved by the authors' ability to "put real lives, names, and faces on the statistics we'd all been hearing about throughout the eighties; people who all their lives had played by the rules, done the right thing, and had come up empty." Lying awake at night, he wondered, "What if the craft I'd learned was suddenly deemed obsolete, no longer needed? What would I do to take care of my family? What wouldn't I do?"

It is the consistent attention to detail that gives these songs their particular resonance. The steel industry in Youngstown, Ohio, for instance, had sustained the regional economy there since the early years of the nineteenth century. When the last blast furnace was shut down in 1980 by the Lykes Corporation, the local unemployment rate rose to more than 30 percent. Following the plant's shutdown, the city lost nearly a quarter of its population. Like "Johnny 99," its direct precursor, "Youngstown" offers a glimpse of the damage done to a workingman's identity by the vagaries of an economic system that respects neither history nor community. While Ralph in "Johnny 99" snaps, here the narrator merely sinks.

> *From the Monongahela valley*
> *To the Mesabi iron range*
> *To the coal mines of Appalachia*
> *The story's always the same*
> *Seven hundred tons of metal a day*
> *Now, sir, you tell me the world's changed*
> *Once I made you rich enough*
> *Rich enough to forget my name*
>
> *In Youngstown*
> *In Youngstown*
> *My sweet Jenny, I'm sinkin' down*
> *Here, darlin', in Youngstown*

On the album's title track Springsteen turns on his past. In "The Ghost of Tom Joad" the "highway" is once again "alive tonight." Unlike 1973's "Seaside Bar Song," in which the phrase is followed by "so baby do not be frightened," "The Ghost of Tom Joad" asserts that "Nobody's kiddin' nobody about where it goes." With "families sleepin' in their cars in the Southwest / No home no job no peace no rest," the road is a movable prison. These people are internal refugees from a society that wishes they would just disappear.

If *Born in the U.S.A.* caught, however inadvertently, a certain cultural and historical wave in American history, *Tom Joad* battered itself up against one. Reaganism had succeeded in moving the political center of gravity well to the right of where it had been a decade earlier, and by the mid-1990s most Americans believed themselves to be living in an extremely prosperous and providential nation — a feeling that accounted for Bill Clinton's solid reelection in 1996. Clinton's political success was due, at least in part, to his willingness to abandon the poor as the Democratic Party's traditional constituency. He was consistently praised by the political establishment and national editorial writers for embracing those aspects of the congressional Republican agenda most hostile to the needs of the poor and vulnerable. Clinton's willingness to endorse the death penalty, harsh crime laws, a viciously counterproductive drug strategy, and perhaps most important, his so-called welfare reform likewise sent a strong and welcome signal to America's contented political majority. Poor people, particularly immigrant poor people, would simply have to figure out how to make it in America, as previous generations had. Thus, access to food stamps, subsidized housing, local after-school programs for children, emergency medical treatment, and the like were cut or reduced, as funds were increased for building prisons, military-style drug interdictions, and expanded policing of all U.S.-Mexican border sites.

It was precisely these intentionally demonized individuals with whom *Tom Joad* asked listeners to sympathize. In "Balboa Park" Springsteen gives voice to a Mexican male prostitute and drug "mule" who spends his money on sneakers and his own drugs, sleeping beneath the freeway. In "Sinaloa Cowboys," the Mexican-born brothers Miguel and Luis Rosales are forced by the poverty of their circumstances to accept jobs working for drug dealers in California, undertaking the dangerous work of cooking up "crank" in a bath of hydriodic acid. Following an explosion, Luis is killed, and his brother buries him in the desert, kissing his lips as he lays him down. These are the faces, Springsteen is saying, of your "enemy" in the drug war. Take a look in their eyes. Take a walk in their shoes.

Springsteen believed that the record "fulfills the promises that I made when I began" and represented "a reaffirmation of the best of what I do." Critics in large measure agreed. Though many had trouble actually enjoying the record, few could help but admire the audacity of Springsteen's willingness to buck the political and cultural tide. In a worshipful 8,554-word cover story in the *New York Times Magazine*, Nicholas Dawidoff noted that "what sets Springsteen apart from his peers is that he has succeeded in bringing a mature perspective to the music of youth. . . . He has done it. He is an inter-generational rock star with more than an audience. He has a public."

While it did win a Grammy for best contemporary folk album, *Tom Joad* was hardly a smashing commercial proposition for his record company. Columbia tried to skirt the record's dour content with full-page adver-tisements that read, "The Highway Is Alive Tonight" in the hopes of conjuring up memories of "Jungleland." They neglected to mention that it now led nowhere. The record eventually sold some 2 million copies, which had become Springsteen's post–*Born in the U.S.A.* natural fan base by this time.

Following the release of the record, Springsteen un-dertook what many fans had long yearned for: a solo acoustic tour of small halls. Accompanied by only his harmonica and seventeen precisely tuned guitars, he played auditoriums of approximately three thousand seats each, dressed in loose-fitting flannel shirts, baggy pants, and biker boots, with his hairline receding and his tiny ponytail full of strands of gray. One could hardly avoid the impression that he was quite self-consciously dismembering his own myth. The acoustic version of "Born in the U.S.A." he now played could not be mis-taken for anything but an angry indictment of the coun-try that had betrayed its singer.

Not surprisingly, Springsteen's self-deconstruction

set him free. It liberated him from many of the psychological burdens he felt he had been carrying and gave him the permission he needed to lighten up quite a bit about himself. The 1995–96 world tour has been called the "Shut the Fuck Up" tour (or alternately the "Sour Grapes" tour), but these are actually terms of endearment. The former description derives from the short sermon Bruce gave at the beginning of each show. The audience needed to be "very still, not just for the quiet's sake, but they have to be still because the characters are still. . . . The stillness is a part of who they are. It's a part of the way they communicate; the silence is a big part of the way that they talk. So the silence, it's not just about 'Oh be quiet, I'm playing,' it's because in that silence is character." He then added, "If you like singing and clapping along, please don't," a request that later developed into the friendly suggestion "If anybody's making too much noise, feel free to band together and tell them to shut the fuck up." Singing would have been nearly impossible anyway, as he was now outdoing Bob Dylan in the degree to which he "rearranged and recontextualized," as he put it, his old songs. (Springsteen may have been acknowledging this precedent when, in rare performances of *Greeting*'s "Does This Bus Stop at 82nd Street?" on the tour, he sang "interstellar mongrel nymphs" in mock Dylanese.)

While *Tom Joad* was all business, the tour turned out to be part seriousness and part serious fun. Late in the tour Springsteen began lecturing the men in the crowd on the importance of performing oral sex on their women, as he introduced "Red-Headed Women." But he would also address in unfashionably idealistic language the concerns of the album. In Washington, Springsteen sounded very much like the Ford/Steinbeck character himself when he suggested that maybe our "salvation" lay not in what we accomplish individually, but rather as a "collective" society. Perhaps, he added, "Our spirits rise and fall together." Like virtually everyone who saw these performances, I found the acoustic show both captivating and invigorating. It was a most welcome gift after years of watching Springsteen undertake the artistic equivalent of wandering the desert.

Springsteen seemed to enjoy his status as an elder statesman and de facto generational spokesman, happily undertaking a few activities befitting such a title. He performed with the real "new Dylan," Jakob, at Tradewinds. He sang a beautiful "Angel Eyes" in a television tribute to fellow New Jerseyan Frank Sinatra. At the Rock and Roll Hall of Fame he offered up eloquent induction speeches for Roy Orbison, Bob Dylan, and John Fogerty and Creedence Clearwater Revival, jamming with all musicians present in each case. Springsteen also appeared at a pro–affirmative action rally in California and even made a speech this time before singing "Promised Land." That same month he played a small concert at St. Rose de Lima High School in Freehold, New Jersey, where nuns had tormented him years earlier. Springsteen found himself apologizing to the priest who was the school's principal for saying "fuck" from the stage. He also sang a song he wrote specifically for this performance, titled "Freehold." The song recounted his bittersweet memories of growing up, getting his first kiss, and playing music in Tex and Marion Vinyard's living room. A few weeks later Springsteen played another benefit concert in his adopted home of Asbury Park. Bootlegs of these concerts quickly became among the most treasured possessions of Springsteen fans.

Springsteen sightings on the Jersey Shore and nearby became much more common in 1998 as he decided to move his family back east to be closer to their aunts, uncles, and cousins, and so his children might grow up apart from the entertainment industry. In January of that year, he joined Steve Van Zandt, Southside Johnny, and Jon Bon Jovi in a benefit performance for the family of a slain New Jersey policeman. He played his own birthday party at his farm in Colt's Neck. He did another Amnesty gig in Paris. But the big news of that year — when Springsteen himself would finally be eligible to be inducted into the Rock and Roll Hall of Fame — came with the announcement that Bruce was readying the "Holy Grail" of box sets. After decades of pleading by fans, he was finally going to go back into the vault and release some of those terrific songs he had imprisoned since 1972.

Springsteen explained the decision by noting that he was looking "to reconnect with the audience that has sustained me since I was very young. Then, you're very concerned with presenting yourself a certain way. Years later, the pressure's not there and it doesn't need to be so private anymore." He added that he did not see himself putting out much in the way of new music for a while, and he did not want fans to go too long without hearing from him. A direct analogue to Dylan's *Bootleg Series Volumes I–III*, the four-CD, sixty-six-song compilation, *Tracks*, is drawn from the legendary material Bruce had played in concert, practiced in the studio, and never released. Each of the CDs corresponds to a particular recording session and, hence, can be construed to represent the shadow of Bruce's career. Once he made the decision to release it, he commented, "*Tracks* didn't take a lot of thinking. I went in. I found pieces of music that I liked that we hadn't released. I didn't feel I had to arrange them conceptually: I based my choices on what was pretty much finished and what I felt were the best things we had done that hadn't come out." Even so, Springsteen's perfectionism forced him to remaster the entire set with his engineer Toby Scott.

Tracks was a generous gift to fans, freeing favorites like "Frankie," "Loose Ends," "Thundercrack," and many others from their existence in poor bootlegged sound. And some of the songs were genuinely new to everyone. One of the great benefits of the record for dedicated Springsteenologists is the DNA through which one can now track the genesis of Springsteen's obsessive craftsmanship. Lines from "Santa Ana" (previously known to bootleg collectors as "Contessa" or "The Guns of Kid Cole") turn up in "She's the One," for instance, and lines from "Iceman" appear later in "Badlands." Maddeningly, even with fifty-six songs, Springsteen had released barely more than 20 percent of the finished material he had sitting in the vaults, and yet again, "The Fever" and "The Promise" were nowhere to be found.

Still, *Tracks* marked the beginning of a new era for Springsteen and his fans. Having finally gotten to the point where he felt comfortable both with himself and with the professional identity he had forged during a quarter century of music making, he seemed ready to loosen up substantially. Now, not every decision had to represent him or define him, and not every piece of music had to stand for the whole. If fans were upset about the absence of "The Fever" and "The Promise," then, what the hell, he would release them on *18 Tracks*, the single-CD highlight disc from *Tracks* released in 1999. (Springsteen even recorded a new version of "The Promise," a song he had not played live since July 15, 1978, because he did not have a version he liked.) He also published an enormous coffee-table photo album of his career titled *Songs*, which not only features lyrics to all his recorded songs and rare and private glimpses of Springsteen but also many original lyric sheets and Bruce's own recollections of writing and recording each album. Finally came the announcement that had had fans holding their collective breath for the past decade:

beginning April 14, 1999, in Barcelona, Spain, Bruce Springsteen would begin a world tour with the E Street Band, featuring the return of Steve Van Zandt on guitar. Most of its members were now (like Bruce) nearly fifty or thereabouts and had families, and a few had developed important post–E Street careers, but so what? Bruce said, "Let's go," and they were going.

The frenzied reaction to his first tour with the E Street Band in more than a decade proved that the powerful bond Springsteen had forged with his fans during the past quarter century had only intensified. Springsteen had no record in the top thirty, and his biggest hit, "Born in the U.S.A.," was approaching its fifteenth birthday. Yet when tickets for the reunion tour finally went on sale, fans snapped up a record-breaking fifteen shows at the New Jersey Meadlowlands — more than 300,000 seats — in just thirteen hours. Phone lines clogged with fifteen thousand calls per minute as fans bought tickets from as far away as Israel and the Japanese island of Okinawa. One Jersey firefighter even deployed his uniform to skip to the head of the line. (His superiors disciplined him, and the tickets were returned.) Front-row tickets auctioned to benefit KACF earned more than $11,750 a pair, and even the usually staid *New York Times* treated Springsteen's homecoming as front-page news.

Shortly before that fateful announcement was made, on March 15, 1999, Springsteen was inducted into the

Rock and Roll Hall of Fame. It was clearly an important milestone for him. He purchased six tables for his family, friends, and band members. He gave a heartfelt speech thanking by name nearly everyone who had ever helped him, including even guest Mike Appel.

I sat at that event in the balcony watching the band, having worn my tuxedo for the purposes of sneaking out of the press room and into the hall, should the opportunity present itself. It was a small room for Bruce to be playing, and I loved the soulful new arrangement of "Tenth Avenue Freeze-Out" and Bruce's spirited duet with Wilson Pickett on "In the Midnight Hour." But the ballroom of the Waldorf-Astoria was hardly the proper venue for Bruce Springsteen and the E Street Band to begin their reunion tour, with record-industry mandarins paying $2,000 a head hardly the right audience. Fortunately, Bruce understood this as well.

A few days earlier, as he was wrapping up the band's final rehearsals at Asbury Park's Convention Hall, Springsteen sent Terry Magovern outside to talk to the three dozen or so fans who had been freezing on the boardwalk all week, listening through the walls. Terry invited the fans inside for a private show. As Springsteen's children ran around the room with ear protectors on, the lights went down and the band broke into "Promised Land." After the song Springsteen asked, "How you guys doing? You are my first audience. That was some leak in the paper." The band then ran through

"Tougher Than the Rest" and "She's the One" before Bruce called out, "You guys been out in the cold too long, what do you want to hear?" After calls for just about every song he had ever written, the tiny crowd was treated to performances of "Backstreets" and "Bobby Jean," Springsteen's song for Steve Van Zandt. Springsteen then walked off the stage, shook hands with every person there, and signed whatever they offered him.

Back at the Waldorf, Bono was speaking onstage. Knowing that Springsteen had "come home," so to speak, reforging his relationship with his fans and rediscovering the original spirit that had inspired his greatest moments as an artist, made amends for the fact that he chose another wealthy rock star to give his induction speech. Happily, the sensitive Irishman with the beautiful blue eyes came through with the "Born to Run" — or at least the "Pink Cadillac" — of Hall of Fame induction speeches. "In 1974, I was fourteen," Bono recalled.

It was the era of soft-rock and fusion. The Beatles was gone, Elvis was in Vegas. What was goin' on? Nothin' was goin' on. . . . America was staggering when Springsteen appeared. The president just resigned in disgrace, the U.S. had lost its first war. There was going to be no more oil in the ground. The days of cruising and big cars were supposed to be over. But Bruce Springsteen's vision was bigger than a Honda, it was bigger than a Subaru. Bruce made you believe that dreams were still out there, but after loss and defeat, they had to be braver, not just bigger. He was singing, "Now you're scared and you're thinking that maybe we ain't that young anymore," because it took guts to be romantic now. Knowing you could lose didn't mean you didn't still take the ride. In fact, it made taking the ride all the more important.

The "greatest challenge of adulthood," Springsteen once explained, "is holding on to your idealism after you lose your innocence." For anyone who has traveled from adolescence to maturity during the past quarter century, there is no better argument for holding on to one's idealism — and no better companion for the journey — than the man who spoke those words and, through the power of his music, somehow willed them to life.

Say it, say it one more time

— "Tenth Avenue Freeze-Out," 1999 version

Epilogue: Land of Hope and Dreams

Twice would not be the charm.

I was sitting with four friends, having eaten one ticket, at the Count Basie Theater in Red Bank, New Jersey, waiting for Bruce. The occasion was a benefit concert, One Night of Peace, which had been announced exactly at the moment that the "one-more-Bruce-show-before-the-band-splits-for-Europe" rumors reached fever pitch. The Internet was buzzing; friends were calling friends every morning for an update. People were on the lookout for a small Jersey show to brag about for the rest of their lives. The European tour was scheduled to start in Barcelona on April 9, 1999. It was now Saturday night, April 3, which left the band and crew six days to make the flight and get plenty of rest. *No problem*, I figured. When I heard about the Basie benefit, with no acts attached to it, I ponied up for six tickets without a second's thought.

The joke this time was that "Bruce" did show up. Bruce Foster, that is. Imagine a band so annoying that it brings back fond memories of Supertramp. Imagine a show so lame that the highlight is Sporty Spice doing a faux Tina Turner shtick. Imagine driving ninety minutes and dragging four intelligent people to see puppet shows and teenage kid ballerinas do the kind of thing that young parents are forced to see under duress. Now imagine shelling out $216 for six tickets and being excited to do it. Only Bruce Springsteen can make otherwise rational adults behave this way.

I knew I was pushing my luck, but I couldn't resist. Three weekends earlier I had been lucky enough to be present when Springsteen and the E Street Band had played two "rehearsal" shows inside the Asbury Park Convention Hall, and never in human history were 2,500 people happier to be in one place at one time. The city itself looked to have survived one too many near-death experiences. It recalled downtown Beirut back in the days when four armies were invading at once. The famous boardwalk was rotting, and the buildings surrounding the Convention Hall had either never been finished or had been scavenged for kindling.

The crumbling Convention Hall itself was a tacky dreamworld of 1920s bad taste. Seashells, anchors, seahorses, lanterns, and parapets dotted graffiti-scarred walls. One of the replicas of the tall ships placed above the entrance appeared to be sinking into the sea. Desperate for any kind of spark, the city council renamed the block in front of the bar Bruce had made famous, the Stone Pony, "Boss Boulevard." Second prize, quipped *Wall Street Journal* writer Phil Kuntz, should have been two blocks.

Tickets cost $24 each, which went to local charities. They had gone on sale by phone the previous Tuesday and sold out in ninety minutes, though buyers were limited to two apiece. I paid $250 for my single and couldn't have been more grateful. A California man who bought his on the Internet ended up shelling out $2,300 for his general-admission spot, though that money went to charity, too. Dozens of unhappy people were scouring the windswept boardwalk trying to find someone willing to part with a ticket for anywhere from $500 to $2,000 and finding no takers. A *New York Times* reporter interviewed one couple who had flown sixteen hundred miles from Houston with their kids and waited in the freezing-cold line the entire day, "huddling together like dust-bowl refugees," hoping for a last-minute "ticket drop" without ever getting in. Inexplicably, the man, a forty-five-year-old airline executive, told the reporter that he was "having a blast" even without seeing the show.

Once inside the hall, the blessed elect among us took our spaces on the hard linoleum floor without any of the pushing or even crowding that is almost always a feature of festival-seating concerts. Most of us, it turned out, with our thinning hair and expanding waistlines, were too old for that nonsense. In any case, the place was so tiny that territorial stakeouts seemed beside the point. We were seeing Bruce in a room the size of a high school gym. Why fight about it?

The band came on at 7:35. Bruce called the show a "rededication" and let us know that after twenty-five years, "once again, we are at your service." They then played two hours and forty minutes of music that filled every crevice of that small hall with rock 'n' roll so powerful and majestic, it grabbed your soul out of your body and scrubbed it clean before putting it back. From the opening harmonica of "Promised Land" — which had also opened their minishow at the Rock and Roll Hall of Fame earlier that week — decades melted away, fears were forgotten, tempers soothed, and communities reunited. We understood that, for the next few hours anyway, all would be right with the world. Bruce was now forty-nine, with thinning hair and biceps that were not nearly as tight as they had been a decade earlier, but the muscles on the world's greatest rock ensemble were only beginning to flex. With four guitars, two keyboard players, Clarence Clemons's soaring sax solos, and a much-improved "Mighty" Max Weinberg — fresh from playing every night with Conan O'Brien for five years — they formed a musical locomotive that barreled through the Springsteen songbook at the speed of sound. "I have been reborn, rededicated, resusciated, reinvigorated, and rejuvenated with the majesty, the mystery, and the ministry of rock and roll," Springsteen screamed from the stage. So, too, had we.

The old treasures were there, including "Spirit in the Night," "For You," "Born to Run," "Thunder Road," "Backstreets," and the like. When Springsteen forgot the lyrics to "Badlands," the crowd helped him out. But it was hardly a "golden oldies" show. Old songs were re-worked and new ones introduced. "The River" started out as a jazz meditation, with Clemons playing a mourn-ful Ben Websterish solo. "Tenth Avenue Freeze-Out" had metamorphosed into a kind of old-fashioned soul re-vival, as Bruce called out, "Say it, say it one more time / Everybody form a line." Midway through, the entire band left the stage and Springsteen reappeared, sitting at the piano, and played a flawless version of "The Promise," which he dedicated "to you die-hard fans out there." He told the audience a story of having seen the Who, Herman's Hermits, and the Blues Magoos in this very hall when he was just fifteen. "The Who broke up all their instruments; we wanted to go backstage to see if we could salvage any of that shit." He also pointed to the side bleachers and announced, "I sat right over there when I saw the Doors here." In the middle of the hard-rocking "Light of Day," he trotted out his old Baptist preacher act, listing all the cities he traveled to, deliver-ing his message of redemption, reminding everyone that this is all one country and most of us all want pretty much the same thing: "I cannot promise you everlasting

273

life," Reverend Springsteen roared. "But I can promise you life right now!"

Toward the end of the show Springsteen recast the beautiful love song "If I Should Fall Behind (Wait for Me)" into a pledge of lasting friendship, by inviting not only Patti Scialfa but also Clarence Clemons, Nils Lofgren, and Steve Van Zandt to sing verses alone in the spotlight. More shivers all over. The concert ended with all six mobile members of the band lined up at the front of the stage, playing with what looked very much like reckless abandon but was actually an irresistible combination of disciplined professionalism and sheer joy. Springsteen had split up the band eleven years earlier, and the irrepressible Steve Van Zandt, decked out in his gypsy guitarist garb rather than the suits befitting his newfound status as a TV star (playing a hired killer on *The Sopranos*) had not played in the band since 1981. He had been its musical motor back then, and his presence this night gave an added emotional jolt to the music he had helped inspire. Everyone looked overjoyed to be back onstage with the man who had made it all possible. "I don't know what to say," Bruce added, "except that I'm real happy."

The final song was a new one, but it sent the crowd home with goosebumps. Based on an old folk song called "This Train" that Woody Guthrie had often performed, "Land of Hope and Dreams" somehow seemed to encapsulate twenty-five years of Springsteen songwriting; twenty-five years that taught many lessons, but one above all: it ain't no sin to be glad you're alive.

Land of Hope and Dreams

Grab your ticket and your suitcase, thunder's
    rolling down the tracks
Don't know where you're goin', sky is turnin'
    black
Well, darlin', if you're weary, lay your head upon
    my chest
We'll take what we can carry and we'll leave be-
    hind the rest

Big wheels rolling through fields where sunlight
    streams
Meet me in a land of hope and dreams

Well, I will provide for you and I will stand by
    your side
You'll need a good companion, darlin', for this part
    of the ride
You leave behind your sorrows this day at last
Tomorrow they'll be sunny skies and all this dark-
    ness past

Big wheels rolling through fields where sunlight
    streams
Meet me in a land of hope and dreams

This train carries saints and sinners
This train carries losers and winners
This train carries whores and gamblers
This train carries midnight ramblers

It Ain't No Sin to Be Glad You're Alive

This train carries brokenhearted
This train carries souls departed
This train dreams will not be thwarted
This train faith will be rewarded
This train carries fools and kings
This train hears the big wheels singing
This train bells of freedom ringing

"Tell everyone we'll be seeing them this summer," Springsteen promised as he waved good-bye. "There's a bi-i-i-g train comin' down the tracks."

The world's greatest rock 'n' roll band was going back on the road.

Afterword: American Skin

In the early summer of 2000, as the two-year reunion tour of the E Street Band was winding to its close in Atlanta before a climactic ten-night stand at New York's Madison Square Garden, Bruce Springsteen introduced a new song to his audience called "American Skin (41 Shots)." The song illuminated the tragedy of the fatal shooting of forty-one bullets into an unarmed immigrant street vendor from the African nation of Guinea-Bissau by four New York City policemen. The song was brutal, as befit its horrific subject. While painful for any parent to hear, the lyrics are ultimately eminently empathetic to all sides. In the song's first verse, sung from the officers' perspective, a panic-stricken policeman hopes and prays he has not made a fatal mistake:

> *Across this bloody river to the other side*
> *41 shots they cut through the night*
> *You're kneeling over his body in the vestibule*

Praying for his life
Is it a gun?
Is it a knife?
Is it a wallet?
This is your life

But when the voice switches to that of the victim's mother, it becomes clear that what looked like a terrible mistake to the white officers looks like a fact of life from the other side of one's "American skin."

Elena gets her son ready for school
She says, "Now on these streets, Charles
You got to understand the rules
Promise me if an officer stops you'll always be polite
Never ever run away and promise Momma you'll
    keep your hands in sight"
'Cause is it a gun?
Is it a knife?
Is it a wallet?
This is your life
It ain't no secret
It ain't no secret
No secret, my friend
You can get killed just for living in your American
    skin

At the moment of its first performance, the two Atlanta audiences were still the only people to actually have heard the song, as it had not been recorded or released in any fashion. Yet it somehow led the head of New York City's Patrolmen's Benevolent Association, a man named Patrick Lynch, to conclude that Springsteen had callously and carelessly impugned the character of those brave men and women who compose what the tabloid newspapers invariably call "New York's finest" (or in its more dated formulation, "the boys in blue"). Lynch promptly went on the offensive, announcing to the media, "I consider it an outrage that he [Springsteen] would be trying to fatten his wallet by reopening the wounds of this tragic case at a time when police officers and community members are in a healing period." Bob Lucente, president of the New York chapter of the Fraternal Order of Police, chimed in. "He's turned into some type of dirtbag," he concluded. "He has all these good songs and everything, American-flag songs and all that stuff, and now he's a floating fag."

These comments were all that was needed for the New York news media to go into the kind of feeding frenzy they appear to require in order to keep breathing. The top cops' attacks on "the Boss" were suddenly front-page news. The *New York Post* led the pack, per usual, but the other tabloids, *Newsday* and the *Daily News*, along with a bevy of local television stations, soon joined the act. Eventually, so did the nation's national newspapers and network news stations. By the time of Springsteen's performances at Madison Square Garden roughly ten days later, the circus had grown so large and foolish as to boggle the mind. For longtime Springsteen fans who remembered the flap over Ronald Reagan and "Born in the U.S.A." it was hard to avoid thinking of George Santayana's clichéd observation as history unfolded a second time as farce.

At the height of the frenzied folly, a sensible student of the media might have argued that the PBA's anti-Springsteen campaign raised a few semi-legitimate questions bearing further investigation on an extremely slow news day. Among these were:

1. Had Mr. Lynch or Mr. Lucente actually heard the song performed?

   Simple answer — no.

2. Did Springsteen write the song to "fatten his wallet"?

   Lynch, for the record, picked a particularly unfortunate symbol here, given that Mr. Diallo was actually murdered in the act of trying to show the officers *his* wallet. In fact, Springsteen did not stand to make any money on the song; all 200,000 tickets for the Madison Square Garden shows had sold out immediately, many months before the song was released. At the time, he had no new records, videos, or anything else to promote, just a two-year tour to finish.

3. Did the Diallo family consider the song exploitative?

   Amadou's parents, Saikou and Kadiatou Diallo, asked to meet Springsteen at the show. "I asked to go and see him. He didn't invite me. I wanted to greet him and thank him for the song. I hugged him. I shook his hand. I blessed him," Saikou Diallo said. "He also has children, like myself. He felt it." Kadiatou Diallo explained that she appreciated Springsteen's song about her son because "it keeps his memory alive."

4. Were the police spokespeople genuinely representing the views of their constituencies, or merely mouthing off on their own?

This question is the toughest to answer, as it requires a serious inquiry into the attitudes of a representative sampling of tens of thousands of police, something no one even attempted. While much of the police brass did appear to support Lynch, this turned out to be of questionable political value. Mr. Lucente, of "fucking dirtbag" and "floating fag" fame, was quickly forced to apologize and soon resigned from the force entirely. New York's volatile mayor, Rudolph Giuliani, and the city's police commissioner, Howard Safir, joined in, too, though New York governor George Pataki refused, citing his admiration for Springsteen the artist. George Molé, a police lieutenant, wrote an op-ed article in the *New York Times* attacking Springsteen. A former fan who used to play "Drive All Night" for his girlfriend on his car stereo felt betrayed. He wrote, "I didn't expect that Bruce Springsteen, poet of the working class, would turn his back on the working men and women who wear the shield. . . . I can no longer relate to an artist who in his work shows contempt for me and my fellow officers." In reply, a police lieutenant named Michael Gorman penned an eloquent letter arguing that "artists are not supposed to follow strict political lines. . . . Mr. Springsteen has generally been a supporter of police officers, giving generously to police charities. Attacks on him are not only unfair but also counterproductive."

Indeed, Lynch and company picked a decidedly inopportune target in Bruce Springsteen. In 1998 Springsteen and his friends did a benefit performance that raised $100,000 for the widow and children of a New Jersey cop, Sergeant Patrick King, who was killed in the line of duty. King's widow, Maureen, was quoted as saying, "Bruce came to the aid of myself, my family, and the police department. I'll never forget that. He is a very caring and generous person." And, yes, during some of the shows I attended, men who appeared to be off-duty cops booed obnoxiously during the song's performance. Yet during the rest of the songs, these same fellows seemed to cheer as enthusiastically as the rest of us. In six attempts, I could not identify a single police officer trying to get rid of his tickets. So the only sensible answer to question four is, We have no idea.

Unfortunately, admitting to ignorance about questions of alleged public import is not in the job description of most members of the media punditocracy. Their task is to talk—or write—regardless of knowledge, evidence, or, in this case, common sense. And this they did with a degree of enthusiasm and ignorance that surprised even their most hardened and cynical critics, including myself. Apparently on the basis of collective clairvoyance, the members of the punditocracy came up with the following set of explanations for Springsteen's alleged motivations:

- Timothy Noah, filing from the intellectual prison of "InsidetheBeltway," Washington, D.C., for the on-line magazine *Slate*, guessed that Springsteen had written the song in hopes of helping Hillary Clinton with her Senate race before Mayor Giuliani got out. He ventured this despite the fact that Springsteen has never said a word, good or bad, about Hillary Clinton, had repeatedly refused invitations to the White House to visit the Clintons, did not live in New York (where the election was taking place), and claims not to have even voted since 1972.

- John Tierney of the *New York Times* wrote that Springsteen wrote "American Skin" because he has "joined ranks with limousine liberals. . . . Besides his current anthem against police brutality, he has been crusading to preserve affirmative action pro-grams, not exactly a popular cause in his old neigh-borhoods. The singer who recorded 'Greetings from Asbury Park' seems to have made an ideological crossing of the Hudson: Greetings," he quipped, "from Central Park West."

- Paul Mulshine of the *Newark Star Ledger*, who has never known Springsteen personally, somehow professed to know that Springsteen wrote "American Skin" because "situations involving potentially violent felons, loaded guns and dark vestibules scare the hell out of [him]—he just won't admit it." Revealing more about himself than about the artist, Mulshine explained, "We suburban guys are not quite up to the challenges of the city streets. In my case, this is no problem. I'm not pretending to be the boss of anything except that little patch of lawn that serves as a buffer between me and the real world. But Bruce has spent his life trying to convince the world he's a tough guy from Jersey. He's not."

• In by far the nuttiest of attacks, Steve Dunleavy of the *New York Post* explained that Springsteen wrote "American Skin" because "he wants to act as some kind of court of appeals." Think, he continued: "Does anyone believe that a Frank Sinatra or Tony Bennett or a Sammy Davis Jr. would resort to these kind of lyrics?" Well, er, no. Of course, none of those guys ever wrote a single song himself, and in Sinatra's and Davis's case, they spent a lot of time with the guys who were running organized crime—presumably genuine enemies of law and order—and occasional cop killers, but never mind.

The song became an occasion for a kind of free-for-all for anyone with a gripe against the cops or even New York City's emotionally flamboyant mayor. The Reverend Al Sharpton told reporters, "We were all born in the USA," and, "No one can tell us we can't stand up for what is right." Sharpton invited Springsteen "to march with us to Washington, where we all will stand up against police brutality." Jimmy Breslin used the song as a stick with which to beat up Mayor Rudy Giuliani. "At the last hour," he wrote, "only Bruce Springsteen comes in to remind this city of its duty never to forget a horror."

Note that none of the pundits or politicians making any of these claims had yet—or perhaps has ever—heard the song. The first time I did, on opening night at the Garden in the presence of the Diallos, I was deeply moved by its quiet, mournful dignity as I tried to imagine the pain a parent must feel upon hearing such horrific news. Springsteen usually asked for quiet as the band began its chant of "forty-one shots." Screams of various types, pro and con, quickly muted into a kind of hush as the song's quiet power began to pulse through the veins of the crowd. As one critic would write, "With piano chords tolling behind Mr. Springsteen's care-worn voice," the song is "a resonant elegy and a reflection on how fear can become deadly." Springsteen made no statement beyond the song itself.

Springsteen and his organization remained mute throughout the entire uproar. On opening night, as the controversy was reaching its weird crescendo, he opened the show with a new rocker called "Code of Silence," co-authored with Joe Grushecky. His decision to open with it was quite ambiguous: for the song's lyrics might be about a couple that can no longer communicate—there's a "darling" and a "baby" in there—or it might be about the betrayal of a public trust, as when police officers protect one of their own wrongdoers owing to a misguided code of loyalty that trumps all other issues of justice. The latter interpretation would have constituted a pretty effective response to those who accused Springsteen of exploiting—rather than exploring—the tragedy.

The hullabaloo took forever to die down, as others rushed to cash in on its prominence. One of the most inventive of these was Stephanie Fix, a musician from New Paltz, New York. When Springsteen fans using Napster downloaded a file called "Bruce Springsteen American Skin (41 Shots) Studio Version.mp3," they discovered that they had instead pirated a recording of "Bitterfool" by Stephanie. The scheme, masterminded by John Fix, Stephanie's brother-in-law and technical adviser, was said to attract four or five hundred downloads a day.

In another strange tributary to the story, the *New York Post*, demonstrating the commitment to reliability for which it is so justly famous, published a highly detailed, albeit entirely false, report of Bruce's grabbing cops to walk around the Garden with him and arrest ticket scalpers. The story snidely noted that "the cops' anger at the Boss apparently didn't stop them from enforcing anti-scalping laws." Of course, it may have, but we will never know, as the story was wholly made up. (To my knowledge, there was no correction printed, as this would have contradicted its point regarding the artist's reliance on the very same policemen he allegedly defamed.)

In the end, the arguments and counterarguments could

not obscure the triumph that was the E Street Band's two-year reunion tour. Playing 134 shows at $67.50 per ticket and raking in hundreds of millions of dollars, the band quickly jelled back into the most exciting rock revue that anyone has ever seen. While the shows varied slightly in song selection, their quality ran the gamut from "pretty great" to "incredibly great." One critic, writing in the *New York Times* of the final shows, noted that Springsteen performances at this late date in his history did not merely entertain but also "gave fans a chance to remember their better selves by experiencing music that's all about rescuing meaning from the mundane." Indeed, nothing in music compares to the experience of that musical machine running on all eight cylinders for three straight hours. And the fans I witnessed, ranging in age from eight to about eighty, danced and sang and cried and rocked through the night as if time itself were standing still in tribute.

At the end of the year, "American Skin (41 Shots)" made any number of critics' "Best Of" polls, a decided first for a song that had yet to be officially recorded or released. Springsteen also gratefully accepted a "humanitarian" award from a local New Jersey chapter of the National Association for the Advancement of Colored People, telling the assembled that he had always felt himself "empowered" by music as a boy and that, while he did not feel worthy of the word *humanitarian*, he hoped his music might "embody some of those same ideals." In what appears to be his only public comment on the controversy, the artist also took the rather odd step of penning a letter to a local newspaper in upstate New York called *Artvoice*, which he may or may not have meant for publication. (The newspaper did publish the letter, which was verified as genuine, but quickly removed it from its web site.) After thanking the paper for its coverage of the controversy, Springsteen put the entire strange controversy in perspective:

I was somewhat surprised at the song's response. For me it was just my latest installment of the work I've been doing and the questions I've been asking most of my work life. As "Americans" who are we? What kind of country do we live in, do we want to live in? I always assume there's an audience out there willing to think deeply about the ideas in the work I do. It's one of the things that keeps me probably closer to the heart of what we're about—we "Americans." Thanks for listening.
BRUCE SPRINGSTEEN, Rumson, New Jersey

Eric Alterman
May 2001

A Note on Sources

Much of the factual material in this book was derived from and cross-checked among the following sources: Bruce Springsteen, *Songs*; John Duffy, *Bruce Springsteen: In His Own Words*; *Backstreets* magazine, nos. 1–62 (P.O. Box 51225, Seattle, WA 98115 or www.backstreets. com); Dave Marsh, *Born to Run: The Bruce Springsteen Story*, vol. 1; Dave Marsh, *Glory Days: The Bruce Springsteen Story*, vol. 2; Bruce Springsteen, *The Rolling Stone File: The Ultimate Compendium of Interviews, Articles, Facts and Opinions from the Files of Rolling Stone*; Fred Goodman, *The Mansion on the Hill: Dylan, Young, Geffen, Springsteen and the Head-On Collision of Rock and Commerce*; Jim Cullen, *Born in the U.S.A.: Bruce Springsteen and the American Tradition*; Daniel Cavicchi, *Tramps Like Us: Music and Meaning Among Springsteen Fans*; Marc Eliot with Mike Appel, *Down Thunder Road: The Making of Bruce Springsteen*; Robert Hillburn, *Springsteen*; and Peter Gambaccini,

A Note on Sources

Bruce Springsteen. For information on the early Springsteen years, I consulted the now defunct fan magazine *Thunder Road* and Peter Knobler's fine articles in *Crawdaddy*. Other important material derived from Springsteen interviews published in *Musician, Mojo, Q, The Advocate, New Musical Express, Melody Maker, Addicted to Noise, Playboy, Trouser Press, Creem, Hit Parader, Guitar World, Record Collector, Time, Newsweek,* and the *New York Times Magazine* and broadcast on MTV, VH-1, the BBC, NBC News, *60 Minutes,* and *The Charlie Rose Show.* The published work of many thoughtful rock critics, journalists, and academics was also most helpful. Most of these are identified in the text. Most of the information about the culture and politics of the seventies, eighties, and nineties is drawn from my own memories, from the sources cited in the text, or from one of my first two books, *Who Speaks for America? Why Democracy Matters in Foreign Policy* and *Sound and Fury: The Making of the Punditocracy.* Original statistical sources can be found in the appropriate footnotes of those works.

Acknowledgments

Rick Kot is everything an editor should be, but handsomer. It's hard to believe the word *mensch* existed before Rick did, but I am grateful to know such a fine specimen. I have had other agents before, but I never really knew what they could accomplish until I found Tina Bennett. She is the hardest-working woman in the book business, and I feel both honored and fortunate to have her working with me. My gratitude as well to the New America Foundation in Washington, D.C., for their help with research funds and freeing up of some of my time.

One of the most amazing aspects of writing a book on Bruce Springsteen is that people you've never met — and maybe never will — volunteer their time and efforts to help you. I have never felt luckier than when I discovered the talents of two young people, so young they were not even born yet when *Born to Run* was released, who fall into this category, Eli Lehrer and Christine Vaccarro. In addition to being one of the most poised and charming young people I have ever met, Eli is a veritable Rain Man of Springsteen arcana. His hard work saved me from countless errors and added some extremely shrewd insights. Christine, meanwhile, is also a sharp and knowledgeable critic, as well as a brilliant line editor. Her thoughtful comments are reflected, literally, on every page of this book. I cannot imagine that I have ever done anything to deserve the contribution to this work I received from these two wonderful young people.

But that's not all. I've never met Tom Bernardo, a recent graduate of Notre Dame Law School, but I would like to thank him in person someday for the all the research help he so gallantly offered me. Ditto Lauren Onkey. Her amazing files — copied at her own expense and sent to me — provided a wealth of material of which I might otherwise never have known. Jodi Peckman was great about helping me track down photographs. Thanks also to Colette Olry de Labry for reasons that I'm afraid will have to remain as mysterious as her name.

Three terrific photographers — also people I've never met — were generous enough to contribute their pictures to me just because they wanted to help. You can see the talents and generosity of Judi Johnson and Phyllis and Chris Rogers on the appropriate pages of the book. Thanks to Ann Leib for help with tickets, and to Michele Stadnik for helping me come up with the title.

Kevin Kinder deserves the gratitude of many for keeping "LuckyTown Digest" going, but from me in particular, for providing so interesting and knowledgeable a forum. Ditto the folks at *Backstreets*. Many of the people on the AOL Springsteen board were also eager to help with questions when I had them.

My friends Beryl Bucher and Laurel Cook offered helpful and encouraging reads of the early chapters of this book. Todd Gitlin tried but failed to win me over on *Human Touch*. George Stephanopoulos read every word of the manuscript and offered many helpful and encouraging comments. Of all the qualities of George's I most admire, first among them is his dogged and unflinching loyalty to his longtime friends.

On October 28, 1976, Diana Roberta Silver and I busted out of class — ninth and tenth grades, respectively — to head down to the old Palladium on Fourteenth Street to see Bruce and the E Street Band for the first time. Twenty-three years later I cannot begin to express my gratitude to this research scientist, doctoral student, literary critic, and mom extraordinaire, for the joy she has brought to my life. Even more, I thank Diana for her starring role in the production of the beautiful and talented Eve Rose Alterman, who is to baby daughters what the E Street Band is to rock 'n' roll. These are better days indeed.

I am sure I have made a mistake or two somewhere in this book. I will figure out whom to blame once I find out what they are.

PICTURE CREDITS

COPYRIGHT PERMISSIONS